HEAD COVERING

A Local Custom
or
A Theological Principle?

Noel Daniel

Edited by
Annie Wilson
(M.A. English Lit., M.A. Urban Ed.)

**Head Covering - A Local Custom Or
A Theological Principle?**

© 2010 by **Noel Daniel**
ISBN 973-1-4507-3976-4

Edited by Annie Wilson
Cover concept & design by John Pulinat
johnpulinat.com

Published by
Noel Publications
8300 NW 77th Street
OKC, OK 73132
Email: luvnoel@gmail.com
Phone: 405-621-0009

Printed at
Thomson Press
Karimpatta Road, Pallimukku, Kochi-682 016.
Phone : 0484-2351143, 2363374,
E-mail : thomson.press@gmail.com

All scripture quotations in this book, except those noted otherwise, are from New King James Version. Scripture taken from the **New King James Version.** Copyright © 1982 by Thomas Nelson, Inc. Used by permission.

All rights reserved. Except for brief quotations in critical reviews, no part of this book may be reproduced in any manner without prior permission from the Author.

Contents

Chapter	Page
1. The Status of Women Before Christ	1
2. A Brief History of Head Coverings	5
3. Key Questions	11
4. Principles Versus Customs	15
5. The Universality of the Message	23
6. The Necessity of Head Covering	27
7. Reasons for the Man's Uncovered Head	39
8. Reasons for the Woman's Covered Head	45
9. The Equality of Men and Women in Light of the Bible	51
10. Liberation of Women	63
11. The Multi-Level Spiritual Truths in the Head Covering	67
12. The Woman's Personal Glory: A Double Covering?	71
13. What Does Nature Teach?	77
14. Practical Aspects: Who, What, and When?	81
15. The New Practice	85
16. Beyond the Head: Appearance, Spirit, and Apparel	87
17. The Place of Women in Church	109
Appendix	133

Foreword

There was a time that women were given only a subservient position in the society, especially among the Jews, the chosen people of God. It is the teachings of Jesus Christ that elevated the position of women in the society. The epistles of Apostle Paul instruct Christian women about their role, responsibilities, and privileges at home, in society, and in their spiritual life. Unfortunately, we live in a world where the new generation is heading in an irreligious direction, questioning and twisting the teaching of the Bible. Many biblical practices of women are becoming obsolete and irrelevant to the modern milieu of Christianity. To eradicate such insidious influences, let the preachers and writers wake up and reinstate the Christian doctrines in the hearts of believers.

Many Christian women are unclear about head covering, dress codes, and their responsibilities in spiritual gatherings. They can be classified into three groups: first, those who are ignorant about the importance of the Biblical teachings, but ready to follow if they are convinced; second, those who do have the knowledge of the Word of God, but neglect to follow it; and third, those who do not believe in practicing the teachings of the Bible, and so blindly refuse to follow them. For example, short hair is a modern trend among Christian women that was not seen even among unbelievers in olden times. It shows that these worldly practices are gradually infiltrating Christian churches. The author of this great book *Head Covering: A Local Custom or a Theological Principle?*, Noel Daniel, has shown immense industry in clarifying and emphasizing the importance of biblical teachings into practice. A few years back, I was moved by the Holy Spirit to write about the incorrect practices in churches, and I wrote more than eight detailed pages on the same issue in my book *Family*.

In ancient times, women all over the world covered their heads, since they lived in acquiescence to male domination everywhere. In the subcontinent of India, women cover their heads even now, regardless of their religion. For example, the ex-Prime Minister Indira Gandhi, the Congress leader Sonia Gandhi, and many other prominent women leaders all over the world have always covered their heads as a part of their culture. Though head covering is related to tradition and religion, the use of head covering emphasized in the Bible is not, but rather is a doctrinal truth given by God for His chosen people.

The Bible specifies that Jesus Christ is the Head of the Church. In the epistle to the church at Corinth, Apostle Paul gives a detailed explanation in connection with the creation of men and women, and a lucid description of the principle of Headship. It says that Adam received headship or leadership directly from God. Because of sin, Adam lost it, but after the death of Jesus Christ on the cross redeemed mankind from sin, all men got the headship back. Jewish men, who do not believe in the redemption, still cover their heads while praying at the synagogue. If a woman comes to church without covering her head, it shows that she is not under the headship of any man.

In the ancient Greek culture, if a woman didn't cover her head in the public, it showed that she was leading an immoral life, yet at the same time slave women had to shave their heads. To comprehend the situation of women who didn't cover their heads, read the detailed elucidations in Numbers 5:18 and Deuteronomy 21:13. If the Bishops of any Christian denomination cover their heads during the service, it is contradictory to the Word of God.

Bro. Noel Daniel, the author of this unique book, leads a very busy life holding two jobs, tending to his family, teaching Sunday School students at church, and in general participating actively in church activities in Oklahoma. Yet God has been using him to write many important books on vital Christian doctrines for the edification of the New Testament Churches. May the Lord bless him abundantly and use his innovative nature in studying the Word of God and conducting research to produce more books for the use of the believers and unbelievers! With much prayer and appreciation, I present this book to the community of born-again Christians and for the glory of God!

Dr. Sunny Ezhumattoor (John Mathew)
Houston
January 11, 2010

Book Review 1

Father guards her at her childhood; husband guards in her youth;
Old age guardian is her Son; thus a woman can never be left alone.
— **Manusmriti, 8:3**

This is a proverb applied practically in the life of women centuries back in India and many other male dominant countries. It was the era when women were completely submissive and defended by a male member in the family, in a widely accepted norm of the ancient society of authoritative men and illiterate women, but in the course of time this pattern of social life has gradually moved behind the curtain.

As time changed, their dress code switched.
That makes hard to make out their gender.
— **Annie Wilson**

This present young generation can be portrayed as a faction liberally moving toward an unknown destination, breaking the barriers of tradition and customs, and because of their similarity in haircut and clothing it can be hard to distinguish between a male and a female. This escalating tendency has transfigured the natural and beautiful appearance of women with their long hair and feminine garb; that means their original womanly look is gone. This may be because of the

"Feminist Movement" to attain their lost equality. Nowadays, women of all levels struggle not only to improve their financial status, but also to pursue various fashions not considered modest in many religions. What if such an inappropriate trend prevails among women in Christian churches who declared their faith in Jesus Christ?

Noel Daniel, a renowned Christian writer and the author of this book, *Head Covering: A Local Custom or a Theological Principle?*, is specially chosen by God and bestowed with a special gift to use the powerful Word of God to persuade and deter Christian women from the ungodly penchant to adopt these worldly practices. The theme of this unique book is very rarely addressed by Christian preachers, teachers, or famous authors. Noel spotlights the imperatives of these unusual subjects according to the Word of God and demonstrates them with a discerning heart and coherent support. This new book shows his deep scholarly knowledge and his thoroughness in researching such unusual topics. Its contents clearly answer the disputed question: "Do women have to cover their heads when they attend assembly gatherings or while praying?"

Using irrebuttable support from the Bible itself, the author proves that a woman has no authority to alter the position that God has bestowed on her. He elaborately expounds his inspirational idea that it is a command of God that women must cover their heads in church with reference to the first epistle to the Corinthians, chapter 11, by Apostle Paul. To emphasize this imperative, he refers not only to verses from the Bible, but also to much other supporting evidence from various sources, such as excerpts of the Apostolic fathers, the differences in creation, the biological and chromosomal distinctions between men and women, the traditional impact of various religions (including Judaism), and the history and influence of customs and culture in various civilizations. I personally do not exclude the possibility of embarrassment among women who wear the head covering on reading that their head covering also represents the fallen glory of man because of the deceived woman and the disobedience of man.

Noel Daniel deserves much appreciation for revealing many facts embedded in a simple head covering which is the command of God.

I'm pretty sure that no woman who reads and comprehends the unshakable truth embedded in this book would ever pray without covering her head. May this book written with the guidance of Holy Spirit be a leading light for its readers!

Annie Wilson (Agnes Varughese)
New Jersey
January 10, 2010

Book Review 2

We have received another informative book from Bro. Noel Daniel, who has enriched Christian literature in Malayalam through his writings. In *Head Covering: A Local Custom or a Theological Principle?*, he explains in detail the propriety of wearing a covering for the head, with Scriptural authority, historical evidences, and ample illustrations.

Inadvertently, Christian women have continued to wear head coverings as if following the steps of Christian women in all generations who used it. Gradually, it has become a tradition with unknown reasons, especially the spiritual implications and God's command veiled in the veil.

About 2000 years ago women had no status in social life. It was Jesus Christ who uplifted them in the society and gave them dignity. It is true that many of the world religions do not offer women appropriate positions in their religion or society, but during the public ministry of Jesus Christ, many women accompanied him and served him and the disciples. Mary called Magdalene, Joanna the wife of Chuza Herod's steward, Susanna, and many others were among them. The early church also did not exclude women from the ministry.

Wearing a head covering does not necessarily mean that women are any less important or that they are showing a symbol of male domination. The author of this book, Noel Daniel, clarifies a very important spiritual truth in very simple language.

Just as we obey the other commands of our Lord, we should also seriously consider the directive for the head covering. This command is given to us on the authority of our Lord and through the inspiration of the Holy Spirit. We must observe it in obedience and submission to the Lord. Women do this in order to reveal that they are saved and redeemed, as the Lord's purchased possession. "God created man in his own image, in the image of God created he him; male and female created he them" (Genesis 1:27). The Lord came in search of the man who sinned and who had lost the God-given glory. The Lord prepared the way of salvation for the man through His Son. It is the declaration of the truth of such deliverance that a woman reveals through her head covering. A woman wearing the head covering represents the fallen and lost humanity and she acknowledges such condition before God. In this manner the veiled glory of both men and women are evidenced and the glory of God alone will shine forth among them.

This is a "must read" book for everyone, especially for the young sisters all around the world, because there are sufficient reasons to doubt the validity and spiritual meaning of wearing a head covering by Christian women.

I sincerely hope and pray that this book will continue to bring glory to God and a great blessing to God's people. May the good Lord help Bro. Noel Daniel enrich the Christian world with many more excellent books!

Mercy Samuel
New Jersey
January 15, 2010

Acknowledgments

The increasing number of uncovered heads of Christian women in church gatherings seems an inadvertent disobedience of the Word of God, and seeing this open negligence of the instruction of Apostle Paul I felt guilty if I would fail to enlighten them with the facts of God's command to wear head covering. I'm greatly thankful to God for inspiring me to expound on the true divine rationale and compose this book.

On realizing the present generation's need for a book with authentic, detailed evidence and clear conclusions on head covering, I first wrote one in Malayalam focused only on the Malayalee community of believers. Within a few months, upon the request of many Christian readers, I translated the Malayalam edition into English. I'm filled with gratitude toward all the believers who instilled me with the confidence to do the translation of Head Covering.

I wholeheartedly thank the famous author and scholar Dr. Sunny Ezhumattoor (John Mathew) for his insightful introduction and his unflagging encouragement in my writing ministry.

I'm greatly thankful to Mrs. Annie Wilson (Agnes Varughese), the well-known linguist and translator who, despite her busy teaching jobs in college and school, proofread and edited this book meticulously, and wrote a profound book review. Her assistance, encouragement, and creative insights greatly enhanced this book, and have been an indispensable support to me in publishing it. In fact, she took the initiative in the translation work.

As always, I thank my loving wife Sheeja and my two children, Nelvin and Elna, who sacrificed their time so I could make my dream a reality.

Special thanks to Bro. P.T. Johnson for his assistance and encouragement in publishing this book. I am also grateful to the hymn writer Mrs. Mercy Samuel for her valuable comments.

I extend my sincere thanks to Mr. Dan McNeill, an award winning, best-selling author at spectrum-editorial.com who professionally edited and enriched this book.

I am grateful to Pulinadan (Bro. John Pulinat) for designing the cover page using his illustrative art and creative imagination.

I hope that the truths revealed in this book will inspire and influence many believers and I commit this book with the prayer that God may make it a blessing for all who read it!

Noel Daniel
Oklahoma
December 25, 2009

Chapter 1

The Status of Women Before Christ

Historical research leads us to the conclusion that the position and value of women were at their lowest state around the world before Christianity was established. Women were downtrodden and discriminated-against creatures, puppets in the hands of men and society. This fact was readily observable among many religions and communities during the first century.

Women in Jewish Culture

By Jewish custom, the primary task of women was to stay home and take care of the household. Women were little esteemed and their testimonies were regarded as dubious. Jewish writings demonstrate the fact:

"Sooner let the words of the Law be burned rather than delivered to women." (Talmud, Sotah 19a)

"Happy is he whose children are males, but woe to him whose children are females." (Talmud, Kiddushin 82b)

One Jewish prayer from that era declared, "I thank thee that I am not a woman."

"Any evidence which a woman [gives] is not valid [to offer], also they are not valid to offer." (Talmud, Rosh Hashannah 1.8)

According to the statement in Rosh Hashannah, a woman's testimony was given the same weight as that of a robber. Josephus supports this: "But let not the testimony of women be admitted, on account of the levity and boldness of their sex, nor let servants be admitted to give testimony on account of the ignobility of their soul; since it is probable that they may not speak truth, either out of hope of gain, or fear of punishment." (Josephus, *Antiquities* 4.8.15)

Women in Ancient Greece and Rome

The Jewish attitude toward women was hardly unique in the first century. Before Christ, women enjoyed few rights and little status in the public mind. It was the teachings of Jesus Christ that granted them dignity and respect later in the society. The Greek philosophers during the time of Christ did not admit women as disciples. Craig S. Keener says in the IVP Bible commentary that "women staying together as a group was a disrespect." It was unheard of that men and women might learn together in the same room at that time.

In the first century, the Romans shared a similar low view of women. The well-known Roman historian Suetonius (A.D. 115) writes of Caesar Augustus, who was the emperor at the time of Jesus' birth through A.D. 14:

"Whereas men and women had hitherto always sat together. Augustus confined women to the back rows even at gladiatorial shows: the only ones exempt from this rule being the Vestal Virgins, for whom separate accommodation was provided, facing the praetor's tribunal. No women at all were allowed to witness the athletic contests; indeed, when the audience clamored at the Games for a special boxing match to celebrate his appointment as Chief Priest, Augustus postponed this until early the next morning, and issued a proclamation to the effect that it was the Chief Priest's desire that women should not attend the Theatre before ten o'clock."

Females were often abused. "Women in Ancient Rome were considered child bearers and possessions and enjoyed very few if any civic liberties," says Molly Carter in *The Life of Women in Ancient Rome*. "Roman women had no real identity, not even an individual name. Because a woman was not thought worthy of any sort of individualism, a girl was given her father's middle name, and the name was feminized. It served to dictate to society exactly what social class she was in and to whom she belonged.

"At birth, a father could choose to recognize his daughter. A woman would place her child at her husband's feet and if he picked her up, she was considered part of the family; if he ignored her, she was either abandoned at the river or left to starve. Because a girl could not carry on the lineage and required a dowry to marry, many baby girls were left to die."

The Influence of Christian Doctrine

The fact that with Jesus women learned together with men and accompanied Him to hear His sermons caused great consternation in the society; nevertheless, women continued to travel with Him and learn along with men (Luke 8:3). Jesus had a public conversation with the Samaritan woman regardless of their differences in culture (John 4). Jesus did not find any fault in Mary, sister of Martha and Lazarus, sitting at His feet and learning from Him; instead, He told Martha to follow Mary's example (Luke 10:38-42). At a time when women were not allowed to enter the synagogue or temple, the first-century church did not restrict them (1Cor.11:2-16). The teachings of Jesus turned the Jewish-Greek-Roman culture upside down.

Frank Morrison says, "The influence of Jesus on the women of His day was profound, and of surpassing interest. He took Mary Magdalene from her native Magdala and made her His bond-slave for ever. He took the sons and breadwinners away from women like Salome and Mary, the wife of Cleophas, yet they would have died willingly for His cause, and did later endure unspeakable hardships on His account. He was the close and intimate friend of cultured women like Mary and her sister Martha. He had in Joanna faithful and devoted follower in the very household of Herod."

Chapter 2

A Brief History of Head Coverings

Head covering for women had been a custom in many countries and religions all over the world for centuries, even before Christianity. They had worn the coverings for various reasons such as social, religious and traditional practices. The civilizations of the two ancient countries, Greece and Rome, are the ancestral to many other cultures, especially those of Europe and North America.

Greek Worship

Corinth is a famous city in Greece and one much discussed in the New Testament where Apostle Paul visited and preached the Gospel. It was a thriving, cosmopolitan city known for its diversity, culture, commerce, paganism, immorality, and wealth. Corinth was reputed to be one of the most beautiful cities of the polytheistic Greco-Roman world, and its residents followed the general Greek custom in worshipping their gods. Among its many mythological deities, Apollo was the patron god of the city. Some Greek men and women prayed and sacrificed to their gods with heads uncovered because of their lack of awe for God.

Roman Worship

The Romans likewise believed in many different gods and goddesses who originated from a mix of different influences. At the time of the New Testament, Corinth was under the Roman rule. So the Corinthians followed the religious customs and practices of Romans. It is known that Roman priests covered their heads in religious ceremonies. Most Roman men and women also used to cover their heads while praying.

Head Covering Among Jewish Women and Men

In Judaism there are two separate practices for head covering, one for men and one for women.

Among women, Jewish widows and divorcees must cover their heads by custom. However, a woman who has never married need not follow this practice.

The Talmud in Kesuvos 72a states that the source for this prohibition is Numbers 5:18, which deals with the laws of a suspected adulteress: "The priest shall stand the woman before God and uncover her hair." Rabbi Shlomo Yitchaki, author of the primary commentary on the Talmud, provides two explanations for the Talmud's conclusion:

1. It punishes her measure for measure for exposing her hair to her paramour.
2. By exposing her hair, we see that under normal conditions a Jewish woman's hair should be covered.

In Judaism, to wear a *kippah* is to proclaim that "I am a proud Jew." The Talmud says, "Cover your head in order that the fear of heaven may be upon you." Humans wear a *kippah* in order to remind them of God, the Higher Authority above them (Kiddushin 31a). External actions create internal awareness; wearing a symbolic, tangible "something above them" reinforces that idea that God is always watching. Scholar David Haley says that Jews should wear *kippah* to distinguish themselves from Christians, especially at the time of prayer. Therefore there are other reasons for Jewish head covering:

1. To acknowledge that God is above men.
2. To obey the Torah.
3. To identify with other Jews.

Is It Right for Jewish Men to Cover Their Heads?

Jewish men have used head coverings in synagogues for centuries. There's no commandment in the Bible for men to wear head coverings. Man has been given authority and responsibility and a man is never to wear on his head a mark of subjection, but Jewish men did so because the rabbis told them to. The Bible nowhere tells men to cover their heads.

The rabbis had misinterpreted Exodus 33. Let us look at the context of this verse. Moses was up on the mountain with God and he said, "Please, show me Your glory." (v.18). God said, "So it shall be, while My glory passes by, that I will put you in the cleft of the rock, and will cover you with My hand while I pass by" (v. 21). God kept him in the cleft of a rock, and Moses saw God's glory as it went by. Then Moses was with the Lord 40 days and 40 nights (v. 28). When Moses came down from Mount Sinai with the two tablets of the Testimony in his hand, he was not aware that his face was radiant because he had spoken with the Lord (v. 29). The glory of God was all over Moses' face and the Israelites could not look at it. So he put on a veil, went down the hill, and talked to the children of Israel.

The rabbis said, "Moses had to be veiled in the presence of God, so every Hebrew man must be covered in the presence of God."

Actually, they missed the whole point. Let us look what the Scripture says: "But whenever Moses went in before the LORD to speak with Him, he would take the veil off until he came out; and he would come out and speak to the children of Israel whatever he had been commanded. And whenever the children of Israel saw the face of Moses, that the skin of Moses' face shone, then Moses would put the veil on his face again, until he went in to speak with Him" (Exod.34:34-35).

Paul corrected this error in 2 Corinthians 3:13 saying, "Unlike Moses, who put a veil over his face so that the children of Israel could not look steadily at the end of what was passing away."

To sum up: Moses did not don a veil to view the glory, but rather he put it on in front of the children of Israel so they would not see it depart from his face. By misrepresenting that act of Moses, the rabbis imposed on all of Israel a sign of submission to wear on their heads. Paul corrected it in the above verse.

The Jews scattered out of Jerusalem and the Holy Land. There are Jewish communities within the cities of the Roman Empire, particularly in Corinth. Jews had grown up in that city and had children. We assume that some of these Jews were saved, so they started coming into the church, and when it was time to pray or speak, they put on a veil.

Men and Women in Islam

In the Middle East, most men wear head covering. The Muslim religion did not start until 600 years after Christianity. The Arab men use the head covering (*gutrah*) because of their tradition and to protect themselves from extreme cold and heat as well as sandstorms. According to Shariath (Islamic law), Muslim women not only have to cover their heads (*hijab*), but their entire body (*burka*).

Political Women leaders

Head coverings have been used by women of royal families of different cultures all over the world to designate their prominence and social standing. For example, Farah Pahlavi (Empress of Iran) and Jacqueline Kennedy, First Lady of the United States (1961-1963), both don head coverings. The British Monarch, Queen Elizabeth II is never seen without a hat. Famous women who wore head covering belong to Christian, Muslim and Hindu religions. Mother Teresa (Catholic Nun and Humanitarian), Benazir Bhuto (Prime Minister of Pakistan, 1988-90, 1993-96), Indira Gandhi (Prime Minister of India, 1966-1974, 1980-1984) covered their heads in all public appearances.

Women in India and the Indian Subcontinent

Most Christian women in India wear head coverings because of their religious and cultural tradition. Christian Bishops do so because of the inherited ancient traditions.

Early Church

First-century church leaders like Irenaeus, Tertullian, Chrysostom, and Clement of Alexandria were clear about the need for women to wear head coverings (See Appendix). Archeologists have found sculptures, etchings, and carvings (particularly in the catacombs) of people in the early church that show women wearing them in worship and prayer.

The Catholic Church

The requirement that women cover their heads in church first appeared as a universal law for the Latin rite of the Church in 1917 with canon 1262 of its first Code of Canon Law. It was removed in the 1983 revision of the Code, which abrogated the 1917 Code. Some have claimed that it is still compulsory, advancing several grounds for their opinion, including the assertion that head covering for women is an immemorial custom (cf. canon 5 of the Code of Canon Law). However, it was never universally compulsory for members of the Eastern Catholic Churches.

Protestant Churches

Among the early Protestant reformers, Martin Luther's wife Katherine wore a head covering and John Knox and John Calvin both called on women to do so. Other commentators who have favored head covering include Charles Caldwell Ryrie, A. R. Fausset, Harry A. Ironside, Matthew Henry, A. T. Robertson, and William MacDonald (See Appendix).

According to 1 Corinthians 11, various Christian women cover their heads only in worship or in spiritual gatherings. Head covering, at least during worship services, is still promoted or required in a few Christian denominations. Among these are some Anabaptist denominations, including the Amish, some Mennonites, the Old German Baptist Brethren, the Hutterites, and the Apostolic Christian Church; some Pentecostal churches, including Church of Our Lord Jesus Christ of the Apostolic Faith; the Plymouth Brethren; and the stricter Dutch Reformed churches. Many contemporary Christians see this practice as irrelevant, and during the 20th century many churches dropped the custom for worship services and the practice of head covering itself gradually disappeared.

Women in America

To gain freedom of worship in the 16th century, 21,000 people crossed the sea to Massachusetts from England. According to the New

Testament principle, Puritan women wore head covering. Fifty to sixty years ago in the United States, it was considered respectful for women to wear head coverings in church and disrespectful for men to wear them there. Nowadays, women rarely wear hats or head coverings of any kind during church (except among the sects mentioned above), although it is usually still considered disrespectful for men to wear a hat in church or while praying. The code of good manners in North America still reflects this tradition, and that is why men remove their hats in court and during graduation ceremonies.

From around 1930, women began to feel uncomfortable in covering their heads and most of the women have become brazen-faced since 1950's. (See Chapter 17, Beyond the Head: Appearance, Spirit, and Apparel)

Chapter 3

Key Questions

When a law or a canon becomes obligatory for people, arguments about it arise spontaneously regardless of its pros and cons. Let us look at some of the questions about head covering in the past.

Is Head Covering Only a Custom?

In the epistle to the Corinthians Apostle Paul instructs the women about covering their heads, but women elsewhere have claimed that it applies only to the Corinthian women of Paul's day and it is merely a cultural commandment. Scandalous women and those who engage in immoral activities walked around without head coverings while respectable women covered their heads. Then it became mandatory for Christian women to cover their heads in spiritual gatherings. Therefore the practice responds to circumstances in a specific time and place, and does not apply to modern Christian women. It has become outmoded. In the next chapter we will discuss this contention in detail and show that this is not an ancient custom, but it is universal theological principle.

Is Head Covering Insufficient and Hence Irrelevant?

The second point of dispute is that the head covering is a veil, intended to cover the head, face, and indeed the whole body. But if a woman covers only her head, she is not complying with the commandment. So it is better not to use head covering at all! The Apostolic injunction on women is to cover their heads while praying because of the implication of doctrinal truths embedded in it. We'll discuss this point later.

Is Head Covering a Matter of Personal Preference?

Some debaters have sought to undermine Apostle Paul's admonition to wear head covering by saying that it is a matter between the sisters and the Lord. If they are convinced by the Lord, let them cover; otherwise it is not necessary. That is, it is simply a personal choice.

Those who distort the Word of God in favor of their own needs are disobeying the injunction of our Lord. It is for our good that we are reminded of the Israelites in the time of the Judges, when each man did what was right in his eyes, and not according to God's Word (Judges 21:25).

Is Paul's Statement Contradictory?

Some claim that head covering is not only unnecessary, but also contradicts Paul's statement that "woman's hair is given to her for a covering." Why mention in verse 6 that "she should be covered" with a piece of fabric when her hair is already a covering? When we discuss this passage later, we will clarify this apparent contradiction.

Is Head Covering a Sign of Female Subjugation?

Some assert that head covering marks women off as possessing lower status. This argument is weak for the following reasons:

1) If the head covering signals female subjection, it is applicable to married sisters only and this passage must refer only to married women. Therefore, unmarried sisters need not wear head coverings.

2) The apparent implication of male superiority or domination, and women's subjugation to all men, is not scriptural and this notion is to be rejected.

3) If the act of covering the head is a means of symbolizing a woman's subjection to all men—whether old or young, spiritually mature or immature—women will not knowingly accept this command placed on them.

The truth is that head covering does not imply male superiority, wifely subjection, or female subjugation to men, either in the married or unmarried situation. We will elaborate on this issue in detail in the following chapters.

■

Chapter 4

Principles Versus Customs

In early 1960's it was hard to imagine that any female would come to church with her head uncovered. If she could not find her normal head covering, she would grab a handkerchief or a piece of cloth. Even in liberal churches, it was expected that every woman would attend with her head covered.

One of the greatest exponents of reformed theology of this century, Dr. R.C. Sproul, says, "In I Corinthians Chapter 11, Paul instructs the women to cover their heads with a veil while praying. That particular apostolic adjunction was the practice of the church for nearly 2000 years before it was set aside."

Apostle Paul points out that head covering is the sign of subordination of a woman to a man, but among modern Christians it is deemed an outmoded custom. Is head covering for women truly just a custom or is it a true theological principle? The question has become a matter of dispute.

Dr. Sproul suggests that we can take basically four different approaches to the text of 1 Corinthians 11: It is pure custom, pure principle, partial principle, or a merger of custom and principle.

1. Pure Custom

First, we can understand the instruction given by Apostle Paul as deriving completely from the local custom of Christian women in the first century. Hence the matter is arbitrary, and head covering has no relevance whatever to the life of church today. A woman can cover her head with a veil, hat, towel, handkerchief, or nothing at all.

Moreover, we can interpret the act of covering the head as simply a first-century method of displaying a woman's subordination to her husband in church. Women can show that subordination in many ways, and since the act is mere custom, they don't have to do it by covering the head.

And going one step further: Head covering symbolizes the subordination of the wife to her husband in all aspects of life. But even that subordination was a matter of local custom and is not to be carried across into the 20th-century church. If subordination is mere custom, then head covering must be as well.

Thus, the argument runs, since we live in a different culture from that in which 1 Corinthians was written, it is no longer necessary for a woman to cover her head with a veil; indeed, there is no need for a woman to be subordinate to a man. That is one approach.

2. Pure Principle

The second is that head covering is a biblical principle and everything in this text is of trans-cultural significance. And all Christian women, everywhere and at all times, must practice subordination to their husbands and must express their subjection to man by covering their heads. Moreover, God prescribes the covering of the head and His ordinance is in effect at all times and in every culture. And the covering should be a "veil." If any woman uses a handkerchief or hat, she has violated the principle of this passage (1Cor.11:5-13).

This second viewpoint is uniquely dependent on Biblical principles and doctrine, and hence we have to focus on the significance and ramifications of every detail of the passage written by Apostle Paul.

Between these two extremes, there are two other possible approaches: partial principle and a merger of custom with principle.

3. Partial Principle

Under this view, part of the passage is principle, applicable to all generations, and that part is female subordination to man. An advocate of this point of view would say say, "I believe Paul is setting forth a principle that women must always submit to their husbands and be subordinate in the church. That is what matters, and women can show their subjection in ways that vary from culture to culture. They don't necessarily have to cover their heads." So the principle is female subordination and women can cover their heads or not as they choose.

4. Merger of Custom and Principle

Another approach is to see Paul's instruction as based partly on custom and partly on principle. The binding principle is that women be submissive to their husbands and subordinate in the church. Every culture views the head covering of women as an illustration and symbol of their willingness to submit. Thus, we have two principles: Subordination and head covering. However, the material used to cover the head derives from custom. It can be a veil, a scarf, a handkerchief, or anything traditional. The key principles are subordination and actually covering the head.

Since there are different ways to interpret the text, obviously it is not always easy to identify the right one. Therefore, Dr. Sproul points out five basic principles for determining the difference between universal principle and local custom:

    a) Look for apparent areas of local custom
    b) Allow for Christian distinctive in the first century
    c) Be aware of creation principles
    d) Because of angels
    e) Biblical principle

a. First Principle – Look for Apparent Areas of Custom

The writing of the Bible involved the entire Old and New Testaments, from Genesis to Revelation. It took over 1,500 years on three different continents, with 40 different authors from different cultures and every walk of life.

Dr. Sproul says, "The first principle is that we ought to examine the Bible." We must determine, he says, "if there are particular areas that apparently are open to the application of custom." Let's analyze those things that the Bible treats as custom.

❖ *Languages*

Language is clearly a matter of custom, since it varies so much from culture to culture. It is also very important in every aspect of our life. Dr. Sproul states, "From very early times in church history, there was restriction in translating the Bible because of the fear of losing the meaning by translation. First, Bible was translated to Latin, then from Latin to Vulgate and finally to local languages of the people. We have to note that part of the Bible is written in Hebrew and another part in Greek. The Old Testament laws that were originally written in Hebrew are quoted now in Greek in the New Testament. So it is not offensive or grievous to the Holy Spirit to have the ability of transposing and translating the Word of God by the structure of language. It can be spoken in Hebrew, Greek, English, or in any other language."

❖ *Dress Styles*

In the Old Testament people dressed according to certain styles. In the days of patriarch Abraham, they followed one style. There was another by the time of Roman occupation of Palestine in the first century as the New Testament church was emerging. Similarities remained, but styles had changed bit by bit. It was perfectly appropriate for a New Testament Christian to dress in a different manner from the Old Testament patriarchs. We know that in our own culture, dress styles change from generation to generation, and from culture to culture across different regions of the world. For example, our forefathers never wore the modern outfits used by the present generation. Fashions keep rotating in civilizations and cultures.

But one principle runs through the Old and New Testaments: modesty. If standards of modesty change from culture to culture, we have to be careful, because clothes represent our position, attitude, and values. For instance, it is not provocative for the tribal people, dwelling in the uncivilized jungle interiors of certain countries like Brazil, to run around in loincloths, but it would be scandalous for a businessman to arrive at the office in the same outfit in America. It would be highly provocative and immodest, and the person might even be arrested for indecent exposure. Modesty levels or dress code do change based on the culture and custom, but modesty remains the principle to be followed. It is important for us to examine what we are communicating by particular mode of dress.

Changes in fashion influence women of all categories. Decades back in church history, it was provocative for a woman in America to let her ankle be seen in public, but that is hardly the case today. In modern society, no one counts it as provocative for any reason. Changes in styles can vary from culture to culture and they do in the Bible, but again the principle of modesty prevails. God does not set forth in the beginning of the Old Testament a prescribed uniform that every believer to wear since the time of creation, but He did establish the principle of modesty throughout the scriptures.

❖ *Monetary Systems*

The Bible talks about paying tithes and bringing the money into the treasury of the temple of God in shekels (Exod.38:25-26) and dinarii (Luke 24:41 NKJV). A half-shekel coin was roughly equivalent to two days' pay for the average laborer. The denarius (pl. denarii), a Roman silver coin, was approximately the daily wage for unskilled labor. Monetary units have always differed across nations, so in 21st century churches we clearly don't need to bring offerings in shekels or dinarii rather than rupees or dollars. Rather, we need to look for the *kind* of things the Bible recognizes as customary.

b. Second Principle – Allow for Christian Distinctions in the First Century

Most commentaries on Paul's first epistle to Corinthians state that the mark of the prostitutes in Corinth was the uncovered head. However, the commentators do not say that the reason Paul tells women to cover their heads is that they may scandalize the Christian community by resembling prostitutes.

On one hand, it is perfectly appropriate to research the literary and historical background of any document that we wish to scrutinize. It is helpful to know the local customs in Corinth, but at the same time we must not assume that everything the Bible says reflects the cultural situation of the day. Studying the cultural background can help us understand difficult passages, particularly when the Bible does not provide a detailed explanation.

Apostle Paul tells women to cover their heads not because prostitutes do the opposite, but because the Holy Spirit inspired him to provide the real motive authoritatively. That is why he emphatically states the doctrine of subordination—men are in authority, women are in submission. Then he establishes the basis for it by linking it to the teachings of creation of man and woman (1Tim.2:13-14). If Paul simply said that he wanted women to cover their heads in church and offered no explanation, we might reach other conclusions, such as that the practice indeed arose to distinguish Christian women in Corinth from those living in immorality. Where the apostle is silent about a rationale, we need to dig it out by examining the custom and culture of related era. It is interesting to note that these women went around with their heads uncovered, but Paul say nothing about it. Instead, he says, the covering of the head is not circumstantial, but relates to creation.

If there is anything that transcends the women's culture, it is must be those things pertaining to creation. It makes clear that we are not permitted to substitute a rationale that Paul does not state, or dismiss a rationale he emphasizes in his epistles. If we do so, we blindly violate the text. It is here that our study of the ancient culture can block our understanding. Some people assume that the Bible teaches nothing new or different from the first-century culture. Of course, if we just view the Bible as expressing the prevailing custom of the times, there is no reason to study the scripture at all. In fact, the whole point is that the messages of Jesus and Paul were radical and innovative. If we view them as local custom, we miss their entire nature. Hence we must allow Christian distinctions to be as written in the text of the Bible.

c. Third Principle – Be Aware of Creation Principles

The third principle arises from the creation itself. Verse 18 in Chapter 3 of Genesis reads, "And the LORD God said, It is not good that man should be alone; I will make him a helper comparable to him." Verse 23 says, "And Adam said: This is now bone of my bones and flesh of my flesh; she shall be called Woman, because she was taken out of Man." 1 Timothy 2:13-14 says "For Adam was formed first, then Eve. And Adam was not deceived, but the woman being deceived, fell into transgression." If any religion or culture deviates from these precepts of the Bible, it is opposing the purpose of God's creation of mankind. These principles were not handed down solely for a first-century Christian or a sixth-century Jew or a 20th-century American. They were handed down to all mankind for all time. They go all the way back to the beginning of time. Since God did not create Adam and Eve at the same time, but instead gave women only a secondary position in root of creation itself, these principles are not a historical custom. They relate to the order of creation and no one can ever modify them.

d. Fourth Principle – Because of Angels

As noted, some people have explained head covering in I Corinthians 11 as merely a cultural artifact. In other words, like a language or a monetary system, it applied only in a certain cultural period, and had no intrinsic meaning or value. According to this view, this text does not apply to Christians today. We have to keep in mind that when Apostle Paul specifically says, "For this reason the woman ought to have a symbol of authority on her head, because of the angels" (v.10), angels are not cultural phenomena particular to Corinth, but they are spiritual and trans-cultural beings. (For more, see Chapter 6.)

e. Fifth Principle – Biblical Principle, a Principle of Humility

The final and the most important precept is biblical principle. What if, after studying the Bible diligently and examining the historical background and the creation principles, it remains hard to differentiate between custom and principle? Is there a way to find the truth and make sure about it? Yes, there is. The Bible itself tells us how.

Let's assume a case in which it seems difficult to distinguish God's principle from custom. If it is a principle and one takes it as a custom, the person is neglecting its seriousness and disobeying God's word. On the other hand, suppose it were a custom not meant to be followed forever, but someone mistakenly took it for a principle and obeyed it. Now the person is over-obedient. Which is worse: disobedience to God or over-obedience?

The answer is simple: It is always better to be over-obedient. God does not punish for over-obedience. But He may punish you for being loose with the principles he has set forth before you.

This is the principle of humility. Humility requires us to bow before God. If a question remains whether a biblical passage is principle or custom, the burden of proof must always lie with those who argue for custom. Unless there exists a good, sound reason for treating a biblical mandate as custom, we should always treat it as a universal theological principle. God will honor that attitude.

Do not violate the principle of God. We need to become more confident in handling the Word of God for our edification that we may be always equipped with good work which is pleasing to God.[1]

Bearing these principles in mind, let us look more closely at head covering.

■

---

[1] Most of the ideas in this chapter derive from "Principles against Customs" radio message of Dr. R.C. Sproul, Ligonier Ministries. www.ligonier.org.

Chapter 5

The Universality of the Message

Apostle Paul was inspired to write an epistle to the believers at Corinth to exhort them about the infiltration of a women's liberation movement in the church, and to admonish them for their immorality even after becoming the followers of Jesus Christ. Some women were abusing Christian liberty, demanding their own independence and declaring their freedom in the church.

Background of the Epistle to Corinthians

The epistle to the Corinthians tells us that moral disintegration, improper use of spiritual gifts, deviation from the doctrinal truth, and many other Greek pagan influences had emerged in the church. At the same time, the Corinthians retained a high regard for human qualities and achievements such as wisdom, leadership, intellect, and luxury. Like some modern churches, the Corinthian believers were guilty of living not to the glory of God, but to the glory of man. The Word of God tells us that these are indications of spiritual immaturity and carnality. Although the Holy Spirit bestowed a variety of gifts on them, they abused these gifts as well. As a church, they did not reflect the glory of God.

Paul commences his letter by expressing his gratitude to God for the grace showered upon them through Jesus Christ, their high calling, and the spiritual gifts. He praises the Corinthians for remaining faithful to his teachings, and then deals with their problems.

First, Paul admonishes them for adhering to doctrines tolerant of their wrong views, for following mere human leaders, and for making themselves a public display. Paul corrects them saying: "no flesh should glory in His presence" (1Cor.1:29), and "He who glories, let him glory in the LORD" (1:31).

Second, he addresses their exaltation of human wisdom, knowledge and eloquence. Paul writes, "The hidden wisdom which God ordained before the ages for our glory" (2:7), and "which none of the rulers of this age knew; for had they known, they would not have crucified the Lord of glory" (2:8).

Third, Paul writes, "For the temple of God is holy, which temple you are" (3:16), "Therefore let no one boast in men" (3:21). Reminding them about their carnality and false vision of Christian service, he says there will be a reward or a loss at the Judgment Seat of Christ.

Finally, speaking of his mission, he says, "For if I preach the gospel, I have nothing to boast of" (1Cor.9:16). "Therefore, whether you eat or drink, or whatever you do, do all to the glory of God" (1Cor.10:31).

In the first epistle to Corinthians, Apostle Paul commences his greeting in a way different from his other epistles. Paul says, "To the church of God which is at Corinth, to those who are sanctified in Christ Jesus, called to be saints, with all who in every place call on the name of Jesus Christ our Lord, both theirs and ours:" (1Cor.1:2).

Because of that significant phrase "all who in every place" at the very outset, we can clearly see that Paul wrote this epistle to all assemblies to be obeyed. Indeed, how could Paul have been more unambiguous on the seriousness of the matter?

We realize that Paul addressed the epistle to the Romans to, in fact, the Romans; even so, we gladly acknowledge the teachings as relevant to all believers of all generations all over the world. The second epistle to the Corinthians was written to the assembly in Achaia. Though the other epistles went to assemblies at different places such as Galatia and Philippi, every believer acknowledges that they are applicable to all assemblies of all times.

Whether saints lived in the first century or the 20th, the message is not time-bound because time does not affect its truths. All assemblies in the Church age are to follow the inspired instruction in the epistle, for the following reasons.

A. The Lord's Commandment

To prevent anyone from questioning the universality of its application, Paul explicitly states toward the end of his epistle, "The things which I write to you are the commandments of the Lord" (1Cor.14:37).

Paul is not stating that just the Lord's Supper or the exercise of gifts in gatherings of God's people are the commandments of the Lord, but that head covering (in Ch.11) and the different roles of men and women (in Ch.14) are too. If we accept the scripture that suits our needs and reject the scripture that doesn't, we are disobeying the commandments of the Lord.

Prior to the writing about head covering and other matters of assembly gatherings (Ch.11-14), Paul says, "Imitate me, just as I also imitate Christ" (11:1). This statement points out Paul's authority and the authority behind his writings: the Lord Himself. When Paul says, "Imitate me," we should have an obedient heart to follow his teachings.

B. Inspiration and Revelation from Our Lord

In verse 2 of 1 Corinthians 11, Paul states the source: "Now I praise you, brethren, that you remember me in all things and keep the traditions just as I delivered them to you." Paul received the revelation from the Lord and delivered it to all believers, just as he received other teachings from the Lord.

Therefore, the source of Paul's teaching is Jesus Christ. On many occasions Paul used the words "revealed," "revelation," and "made known" (Gal.1:12, 16; 2:2; 2Cor.12:7, Eph.3:3, 5; and Col.1:26, 27).

Let us look at three special words used by Paul in 1 Corinthians and other epistles:

1) Tradition   (1Cor.11:2; 2Thess.2:15, 3:16)
2) Received   (1Cor.11:23, 15:3; Gal.1:12)
3) Delivered   (1Cor.11:23, 15:5; Jude 3)

In the original tongue "tradition" (*paradosis*) means "something handed down or given over," also translated as "ordinance" (1Cor.11:2). It is closely related to the word "to deliver" (Gk. *paradidomi*), which means to "hand over."

The source of this information handed down may be from man or God. When the Pharisees and scribes asked Jesus, "Why do Your disciples transgress the tradition of the elders?" He answered, "Why do you also transgress the commandment of God because of your tradition?" (Matt.15:2).

In the above references, Paul is referring to the Lord Jesus as the source, and not man. Paul received all his teachings from the risen Lord Jesus, including the Lord's Supper (1Cor.11:23) and the doctrine of the resurrections and the rapture (1Cor.15:3). He then delivered ("handed down") these teachings to the assemblies. The Greek word used here for "receive" is *paralambano*, which means, "receiving from another." The doctrines Paul originally received from the Lord, as a faithful apostle, he delivered to the assemblies.

Paul had received the teachings in 1 Corinthians 11-15 through revelation from the Lord Jesus, and written them through the inspiration of the Holy Spirit, and they are for us to follow.

After explaining the purpose of head covering, Paul asks a question: "Judge among yourselves. Is it proper [right, lawful] for a woman to pray to God with her head uncovered?" (v.13). The meaning is that we need to make our own judgment according to our conscience. It is God's plan for women to maintain that submission, not the plan of men or culture. Apostle Paul refuted that argument by explaining that women praying to God without head covering are disobeying the Lord.

Let us ask two questions of Paul:
1. Why does head covering have to be practiced?
2. Why must women wear head coverings and not men?

Chapter 6

The Necessity of Head Covering

Many of us are unaware of the spiritual truth and significance in the act of head covering for women. Some women cover their heads because they do not want to offend others, some because they are following tradition, and others because they don't want to break a commandment of the Lord. Few booklets on the subject exist in English, and the reasons given are not very clear and sometimes unsatisfactory.

According to Dr. Peter Wee, "Some writers think that the head covering is the symbol of male superiority and domination, and women's subjugation to men; therefore, head covering is viewed as a symbol of wifely subjection to the husband, in which case unmarried women object to having their head covered. If so, there is no need to cover the heads of the Christian women whose husbands are unbelievers."

But we should not think that the head covering is simply a symbol of a wife's subjection to her husband, or a way to distinguish a reputable woman from a harlot, as some commentaries say. If we study the passage carefully, we will see that scripture is very clear about why women should wear head coverings and not men. Every assembly must obey the command as the visible expression of an important doctrine.

As Dr. Peter Wee states, "The command is not just to women or wives alone, as commonly thought, but to both men and women, married and unmarried. The very purpose is given in verse 7: 'A man ought not to cover his head, since he is the image and glory of God; but the woman is the glory of man.' Head coverings have nothing to do with the Church order or husbands' dominion over wives or women's subjugation to men. It is indirectly related to order of Creation of mankind."

According to the Word of God, God made Adam first and created Eve later from Adam's rib. Apostle Paul points to the creation order as supporting evidence for the use of head covering. "For Adam was formed first, then Eve. And Adam was not deceived, but the woman being deceived, fell into transgression." (1Tim.2:13-14). Paul says that the two commands—for women to cover their heads and men to keep them bare—both have the glory of God as their primary purpose. "Therefore, whether you eat or drink, or whatever you do, do all to the glory of God" (1Cor.10:31). Therefore, before continuing with the disputed passage, let us look at the theme and terminology of 1 Corinthians.

"Glory" and "Self-Glory"

Apostle Paul emphasizes that man is the "image and glory of God" (v. 7). The logic might mean that woman is not the image of God, but most scholars reject this view. Thomas R. Schreiner says, "Paul is not denying that women are created in God's image, for he is referring to the creation accounts here and was well aware that Genesis teaches that both men and women are created in God's image."

Gordon D. Fee, a New Testament scholar, also concludes that "Paul's own interest, however, is finally not in man as being God's image, but in his being God's glory. That is Paul's own reflection on the creation of man, and it is the word that finally serves as the means of contrast between man and woman." And C.K. Barrett says, "Paul values the term image only as leading to the term glory."

Two Greek words are used to translate the words "glory" and "to glorify." The first word for "glory" (*doxa*) has no exact English correlate. *Doxa* means "brightness," "splendor," and "radiance," but "glory" is the word used. The verb is *doxazo* ("I glorify") and it appears in 1Cor.2:7, 8; 6:20; 10:31; 11:7, 15; 15:40, 41, 43.

The second word translated as "glory" means "self-glory" or "boastfulness." The Greek term is *kauchaomai*, meaning "I glory" or "I boast." It appears in 1 Corinthians 1:29, 31; 3:21; 4:7; 5:6; 9:15, 16. A word similar to this self-glory is *physioo*, which means "I puff up." This is a figurative way of indicating boastfulness, conceit, or pride, and it occurs in 1Cor.4:6, 18, 19; 5:2; 8:1; 13:4.

These three words often appear in 1 Corinthians. *Doxa* is associated with the glory of God and the glory of man, while *doxazo* and *physioo* refer to self-glory.

The Rose and the Plant: Manifestation and Representation

Woman is the glory of man, not his image. Glory is manifestation while image is representation. J.B. Nicholson Sr. notes in "Head Covering" that we can view glory as a visible manifestation of inward nature. For instance, the glory of a rose plant lies in the flower. There is much more to the rose plant, but the flower manifests its inner truth. The flower reveals the nature.

The glory of God cannot be concealed and that is why man is not to cover his head. Image is not likeness; likeness is similitude. Image is representation. Man represents God as His image and manifests His glory; therefore, he must not cover his head in the assembly. God's glory must not be hidden.

God alone receives the glory and no other glory except His glory is to be seen in the gathering of saints. "The glory of man must not manifest in spiritual exercises, therefore that glory must be covered," Nicholson observes. "No glory but God's is to be seen in the spiritual realm. Thus when the man sees the women's head covered, he is reminded that his own glory is covered there too."

Apostle Paul's burden is that we must live to the glory of God and manifest His glory when we come together for worship and prayer. At this point, we should be aware of the composition of believers' gatherings during Paul's time. The Corinthian congregation may have had Christians of Jewish, Roman, and Greek backgrounds. (It was made up of fallen men and women redeemed by God—God's new creation of Jews and gentiles). Both Roman and Jewish men and women covered their heads while praying, but Greek men and women prayed and sacrificed with heads bare. Now the Corinthian church was 30 years old, and Paul was reminding them to observe the practice that was already familiar in the Christian Church of his day. The New Testament Church was separated from the gentiles and they kept themselves away from all the cultural and religious rituals prevailing at that time. Unlike Jews, Romans, and Greeks, Christians had adopted a practice through the revelation they had received from God.

Finally, Paul envisions the following argument: We never covered our heads before the Christian Church was formed. Why do it now?

"But if anyone seems to be contentious, we have no such custom, nor do the churches of God" (1Cor.11:16). This verse has been interpreted in many ways. Paul is acknowledging that the practice had not existed before. Prior to Pentecost, there was no Church, but after the redemption of mankind, and with the formation of the New Testament Church, the glory of God was fully revealed, and therefore this practice became necessary. To manifest the glory of God, the assemblies now had to practice it. Paul also emphasizes that there is no other means to display the glory of God in spiritual gatherings. From verse 16, it is evident that all the churches at Paul's time except Corinthian church practiced head covering. And we see the evidence of the veil as early as Genesis (24:65).

"Sign of Authority on the Head"

"For this reason the woman ought to have a symbol of authority on her head, because of the angels" (v.10). Now the Holy Spirit leads Paul to say that a woman who is submissive in the assembly should give evidence of the external authority. In Greek, *exousia* means primarily "authority," although other meanings such as "power" and "privilege" are possible. In any case, the word indicates that somebody has authority over woman. Some people interpret it to mean the woman's individual authority, but others relate it to the husband's authority over his wife. Since this is the command of God, it would be more reasonable to think of it as God's authority over fallen man. The term *exousia* appears in many places in Bible, for example, in John's gospel: "But as many as received Him, to them He gave the *exousia* (right) to become children of God, to those who believe in His name" (John 1:12). A well-known writer Hkon Haus says that this is the authority that God has given to a woman to become the child of God. As a female child of God, head covering is a message about her authority, a sign that it is female as distinct from masculine authority.

What does it mean to have authority on woman's head? The New American Standard probably has the simplest, most accurate translation. It says, "Therefore, the woman ought to have a symbol of authority on her head because of the angels."

If a woman is to submit, Paul says, she ought to have a symbol of that submission atop her head. Here, Paul is demonstrating that woman is subordinate to man. That means he has a power or authority over her, or there's one who has responsibility. So she should wear the symbol of that submission. "For this reason the woman ought to have a symbol of authority on her head, because of the angels." Not just because it is the custom of the Corinthians, but because of the angels.

From the verse, it is very obvious that this authority is on the woman's head. Since the woman puts a covering on her head, the authority is the head covering. It cannot be the woman's individual authority or the man's authority, but it is the head covering which is the symbol of God's authority, and this authority is over man. Therefore, in order to differentiate between the glory of God and the fallen glory of man under God's authority, the woman ought to have this head covering as the emblem of God's authority over man.

The question then arises: What do angels have to do with this head covering?

"Because of the Angels"

There are numerous angelic beings in the heavenly realm. Since the creation of man, they have mingled in the affairs of human beings. The writer of Hebrews says, "Don't forget to entertain strangers because in this manner some have entertained angels without knowing it" (13:2). In the words of John Milton, "Millions of spiritual creatures walk the earth unseen. From the beginning of the Bible to the end of the Bible, there are angels everywhere." And as Billy Graham says in his book *Angels, God's Secret Agents*, "I am convinced that these heavenly beings exist and that they provide unseen aid on our behalf."

Angels announced the birth of Christ and gave direction to the shepherds. They came to Jesus at His temptation after He had fasted for 40 days and ministered unto Him. Angels appeared from heaven at the grave and announced the resurrection of Jesus. They are going to come to gather the elect from the four corners of the world.

We are certainly a little lower than the angels. Both angels and human beings are creatures, responsible to God and accountable to Him, yet we differ. The key difference is that they are spirits. "Are they not all ministering spirits?" (Heb.1:14). Therefore, we cannot see them, but they can see us.

When the people of God gather for worship, heavenly or angelic observers are looking down on our assemblies, and they are pleased when the whole assembly reflects the glory of God. Luke tells us that the angels in heaven celebrate the conversion of every sinner (15:7, 10). The angels were also witnesses of God's original creation of the earth. "When the morning stars sang together, and all the sons of God shouted for joy?" (Job 38:7). All these angels were shouting at the creation, so they had to be created before the creation, where the creation ordinance of covenant headship was established.

The 18th-century theologian Frederick Godet says, "According to Ephesians 3:10, they behold with adoration the infinitely diversified wonders which the Divine Spirit works within the Church; that, according to ITim.v.21, they are, as well as God and Jesus Christ, witnesses of the ministry of Christ's servants; finally, that, in this very Epistle (I Cor.iv.9), they form along with men that intelligent universe which is the spectator of the apostolic struggles and sufferings. Why, then, should they not be invisibly present at the worship of the Church in which are wrought so large a number of those works of grace? How could an action contrary to the Divine order, and offending that supreme decorum, of which the angels are the perfect representatives, fail to sadden them? And how, finally, could the pain and shame felt by these invisible witnesses fail to spread a somber shade over the serenity of the worship? In Christ heaven and earth are brought together (John i:52)."

Holy angels assist in worship and wish to see respect for the order of creation, as Paul writes in connection with the Lord's Supper. Although we cannot see the angelic host with our naked eyes, the Bible asserts that they are observing how we worship the Lord (1Pet.2:12). Christian gatherings take place in the presence of the angels and should be devout and orderly. Indeed, it is no wonder that the angels show keen interest in the meetings of God's people, and we can imagine their disappointment when they see assemblies of God's people misrepresenting the glory of God and the glory of man.

While human worshipers do not see the angels, they are nonetheless part of the assembly and they participate in its purpose. The phrase "Because of the angels" points back, at a minimum, to what Isaiah saw in the Temple (Isa.6:1-3). When the Lord opened the eyes of the young man, he saw the mountain was full of horses and chariots of fire all around Elisha (2Kings6:17). Like Elisha's servant, Isaiah's visual perception was so enhanced that he saw the celestial beings called Seraphim worshipping Lord, a scene hidden from ordinary human view. Similarly, when we worship God angels attend us in our assemblies, even though we cannot see them.

The holy angels called Seraphim veil their intrinsic glories with their wings as they worship (Isa.6:2). As Matthew Henry says, "This bespeaks their great humility and reverence in their attendance upon

God, for 'he is greatly feared in the assembly of those saints' (Psalms 89:7). They not only cover their feet, those members of the body which are less honorable (1Cor.12:23), but even their faces. Though angel's faces, doubtless, are much fairer than those of the children of men, they cover them in the presence of God because they cannot bear the dazzling luster of the divine glory, and because, being conscious of an infinite distance from the divine perfection, they are ashamed to show their faces before the holy God."

Most Bible scholars refer to Isaiah 6 mainly to corroborate the thought that the angels are in attendance with human beings throughout worship. Several commentators also think Paul mentions the angels because they have an almost militaristic ordering marked by rank and chain of command. This idea was well-known in the popular angelology of the Jews of that period. It seems that Paul supports it by mentioning "principalities and powers," and "thrones or dominions or principalities or powers" in six different places in his epistles. "Thrones, dominions, principalities, and powers" are class of angelic ranks and hierarchies.

Angels watch and learn the relationship of God to men (1Pet.1:12), and a woman's submission to God's delegated authority over her is an example to angels. On the other hand, while angels are there in our worship, it shocks them when man's glory is displayed unveiled, though it is the assembly's purpose to give glory to God. According to Apostle Peter, we can conclude that even salvation itself is something angels desire.

Ephesians 3:10 teaches that the angels can understand the manifold grace and wisdom of God in the church, and part of this wisdom lies in the roles of headship the Lord has delegated. Holy angels do not sin; therefore, they don't experience grace. Grace is one of the attributes of God for which they need to give Him glory, and to demonstrate His grace He wants them to observe the church. By watching the church, they can praise Him for what He has done to redeem the wicked sinners. Thus, God illustrates His glory and grace to angels through the church.

In the church, the greatness of the supreme God is manifested when

His chosen people obey His commands. The roles of men and women form part of that manifestation. When a woman takes a submissive role, the role she was made for the man, and puts a symbol on her head, she demonstrates the wonderful work of God in the church to the angels. Angels are to obey God's orders, so seeing this excellent example they can give Him glory. The holy angels are in perfect and total submission to God, and we as followers of Christ must be the same.

When a woman covers her head in the assembly, it is a sign of obedience and submissiveness to the holy angels and at the same time it is a reproach and a lesson to the angels who disobeyed God. Their sin is rebellion against the divine order. "And the angels who did not keep their proper domain, but left their own abode, He has reserved in everlasting chains under darkness for the judgment of the great day" (Jude 6). In fact, when a woman covers her head in the church gatherings, she is ministering to the heavenly hosts and becomes an object lesson in submission to divine order and headship.

We see much agreement on this view. For instance, John Wesley wrote, "For this cause also a woman ought to be veiled in the public assemblies, because of the angels—who attend there, and before whom they should be careful not to do anything indecent or irregular."

Similarly, Dr. Sproul writes, "While [Charles] Hodge says that women should conform to the 'rules of decorum' it must be maintained that these rules, regarding the worship of God, are established by God himself, not by the whims of culture. It is proper for a woman to have a symbol of authority upon her head; what that symbol consists of does not matter, but the necessity of the symbol remains fixed even as the authority of man remains fixed....As in all things regarding worship, we must strive to be conformed to be God's regulations in all things, no matter how seemingly things insignificant" (Coram Deo, "The Head Covering Is God's Command," 21 June 1996).

J.B. Nicholson Sr. states, "Just as Aaron is a type of Christ in certain ways, though completely unaware of it himself, and just as the Lord used a little child to teach the disciples a lesson on entrance into the kingdom, although the child was oblivious to his role, so now, though we may be unaware of it, we are under the scrutiny of spirit beings. We are being used by God as object lessons to make known the glorious truths of authority and submission which otherwise would be unintelligible to them. How solemn!"

There are two important things angels really understand and never question: authority and submission. In Hebrews Chapter 1, we read that angels are under the authority of God. They are called "ministering spirits." It says, "The Son is here and the angels are here." To which of the angels has He ever said, "Sit at my right hand till I make Your enemies Your footstool?" It says that Christ became "so much better than the angels, as He has by inheritance obtained a more excellent name than they" (Heb.1:4). So angels understand the authority of God, and the submissiveness of their own service. They observe events in the church so they can see God's glory and wisdom reflected there (Eph.3:10). It is pleasing to the obedient angels to see the man's head uncovered, portraying the uncovered glory of God and the authority God has given him.

It's imperative for women to appear modest and submissive, not just for the sake of public sentiment, but for reverence to a superior spiritual intelligence who would be offended by anything less than submission because they understand it to be the right and due honor to God. We should be a non-offense to the angels, and we need to reveal the wisdom of God in His church.

It was Eve who was deceived and fell into sin. However, Adam bears responsibility for the fall since he is the head of the human race. According to Paul, it is Adam, not Eve, who brought sin and death into the world (Rom.5:12-21). When Eve entertained the serpent's suggestion, stepped beyond the protection of Adam's leadership, and tried to deal independently with the enemy, she was deceived. Angelic beings are spectators of the rebellion, sin, and resulting disorder which came into the first creation. God doesn't want the chaos to happen in the new creation. Therefore, God wants women to be subjected, and symbolically she needs to cover her head as an example for angels. If people can understand the submission of a woman to a man, perhaps the angels will understand the submission of the church to Christ and how God's command is carried out in the church gatherings. Moreover, God is also teaching the wicked angels a lesson in how the church submits to God's authority.

Chapter 7

Reasons for the Man's Uncovered Head

A man's uncovered head reveals God's glory. "Every man praying or prophesying, having his head covered, dishonors his head" (1Cor.11:4). In this verse, the Greek phrase *kata kephales echon* means "having down over one's head" or a covering. Scholars say that the noun "veil" is not found in the Greek, so in all verses concerning the head covering, a gerund or another part of speech is used.

According to Vine's Expository Dictionary, the phrase above means "'to cover up' (*kata*, intensive), in the middle voice, to cover oneself." Strong says it means "to cover wholly, i.e., to veil." Its purpose is not to hide, but to distinguish and signify God's order of headship, as revealed in 1 Corinthians 11:8-9, and the order of creation of woman (Gen.2:18; 20:24).

Let us look at the words in the original tongue. Note that all are variations on *katakalupt*, and that the initial "a" in the first two means "not" or "un-":

akatakalupto	uncovered	(v.5)
akatakalupton	uncovered	(v.13)

katakaluptetai	is covered	(v.6)
katakaluptestho	let (her) be covered	(v.6)
katakaluptesthai	to be covered	(v.7)

A veil is mentioned only in verse 16, (1Cor.11) but with an entirely different word. That word is *peribolaion*, in the phrase *anti peribolaiou* ("instead of a veil"). It refers to the long hair given to woman as a covering. Some scholars believe that this "veil" is a covering for the whole body since a woman's long hair is like one, and therefore that she need not wear a veil. The head covering Paul speaks of, however, is not hair, but rather another covering that the woman puts on her head. Paul says in these verses that the head of a woman is to be covered (v.5, 6, 13), the head of a man is not to be covered (v.4, 7), and the hair of a woman is given to her for a covering or veil (v.16).

Since man represents the image of God in the church, he should not cover his head. Moreover, man is the glory of God. If man represents God's image, then he manifests the glory of God. God's authority cannot be questioned and His glory cannot be covered. These are the two reasons for the uncovered head of man, which will be explained later in detail.

In 1 Corinthians 11:7, Apostle Paul gives the key to understanding the whole passage in this verse: "For a man indeed ought not to cover his head, since he is the image and glory of God; but woman is the glory of man." That is, woman is not the glory of God. But since man is indeed the image and glory of God, men need to reflect His image and His glory.

In the above verse, woman is the glory of man, but not the image of man. Hence she is not representing man, but manifesting. In other words, the woman is made to manifest man's authority and man is made to manifest God's authority.

In the spiritual realm, man's glory should not be revealed and must be hidden. Only God's glory is to be manifested and nothing else. Therefore, when man sees the covered head of woman, he remembers that his glory is also covered, and God alone gets glory in the church. "To Him be glory in the church by Christ Jesus to all generations, forever and ever. Amen" (Eph.3:20).

In the heavenly worship, we see the 24 elders falling down before him that sat on the throne, and worshipping him by casting their crowns before the throne, saying, "You are worthy, O Lord, To receive glory and honor and power; For You created all things, And by Your will they exist and were created" (Rev.4:11). As Matthew Henry observes, in heaven they give all their crowns, glory, and honor to the one who had crowned their souls on earth. They owe everything to him and know that His glory is infinitely greater than theirs and that their glory lies in glorifying God.

The uncovered head of the man manifests the unveiled glory of God and the covered head of the woman manifests the lost glory of humankind (both man and woman). Any man who covers his head in the church is veiling the glory of God and therefore he dishonors the head, where God has chosen to manifest His glory.

Apostle Paul says that covering a man's head is associated with shame. The background of this statement is the Old Testament, where in times of guilt, remorse, or sorrow men covered their heads with a cloth. While David was fleeing with all his servants to escape from Absalom, their heads were covered. "But David continued up the Mount of Olives, weeping as he went; his head was covered and he was barefoot. All the people with him covered their heads too and were weeping as they went up" (2 Sam.16:30).

Similarly, when King Ahasuerus honored Mordecai, Haman covered his head in shame and grief. "Afterward, Mordecai returned to the king's gate. But Haman rushed home, with his head covered in grief" (Esther 6:12).

Another instance occurs in Jeremiah 14:3-4, when remorseful men covered their heads, because of a drought brought by God's judgment. "Their nobles have sent their lads for water; they went to the cisterns and found no water. They returned with their vessels empty; they were ashamed and confounded and covered their heads. Because the ground is parched, For there was no rain in the land, The plowmen were ashamed; They covered their heads." John Wesley states, "As in eastern nations, veiling the head is a badge of subjection, so a man who prays or prophesies with a veil on his head, reflects a dishonor on Christ whose representative he is."

From the above examples, we can conclude that, with man, covering the head is a sign of grief, shame, or dishonor. "Every man who prays or prophesies with his head covered dishonors his head" (1Cor.11:4). But every woman who prays with a covering honors her head. Since woman is the glory of man, when she covers her head in the congregation, she reveals the grief of man's sin and the lost glory of both man and woman.

The glory in the Old Testament was temporary, but the glory in the New Testament is permanent. Moses covered his face with a veil in order to cover the glory of the Old Testament. Since the glory in the New Testament is eternal and cannot be veiled, men should not cover their head. "Nevertheless when one turns to the Lord, the veil is taken away" (2Cor.3:17).

Paul says in verse 7 that since man is the image and glory of God, he must not cover his head, for he will thereby dishonor his head since he will emblematically cover the glory of God, which the Church must reveal. Furthermore, Paul states, "Every man praying or prophesying, having his head covered, dishonors his head" (1Cor.11:4). The "head" here may mean either the anatomical head of the man or the Lord Jesus who is the head of the church. Both would be acceptable, as he would dishonor them both. Since male Jews and Romans customarily covered their head while praying, Paul's injunction would have forced an adjustment on male converts from Judaism and Roman paganism. Such men had to be prepared to discard the old practice and accept the new revelation from God.

Men are to be uncovered, not because they are superior to women, but man is made in the image and glory of God. Therefore, man is the highest manifestation of God on earth. In the words of John Wesley, "A man indeed ought not to veil his head, because he is the image of God in the dominion he bears over the creation, representing the supreme dominion of God, which is his glory. But the woman is only a matter of glory to the man, who has a becoming dominion over her. Therefore she ought not to appear, but with her head veiled, as a tacit acknowledgement of it."

Man is God's glory and woman is man's glory, and the uncovered head of man is the silent witness of this fact. As W.E. Vine observes, if a man covers his head, it is tantamount to covering God's glory and a reproach to His majesty.

When man is said to be God's glory, it means God has made him as representative in order to reveal Him. Man's headship and woman's subjection were God's order in creation. God created the man in His image, and gave him dominion over every beast of the earth and every bird of the sky and every thing that moves on the earth (Gen.1:28-30). Therefore, the male is the appointed authority and majesty of God. That's why Paul says, "Wives, submit to your own husbands, as to the Lord" (Eph.5:22).

■

Chapter 8

Reasons for the Woman's Covered Head

"But every woman who prays or prophesies with her head uncovered dishonors her head, for that is one and the same as if her head were shaved. For if a woman is not covered, let her also be shorn. But if it is shameful for a woman to be shorn or shaved, let her be covered." (1Cor.11:5-6).

Paul says, when a woman prays, she ought to have her head covered—or have it shaved! So if she does not want a gleaming, hairless head, she should have it covered. The verses are crystal clear.

Paul's injunctions to both man and woman go against all existing practices in Judaism and the Gentile religions. Why did only the Christian Churches observe them? It was to express God's glory.

Expressing God's Glory

God's primary concern and our very existence are for God's glory. "Everyone who is called by My name, Whom I have created for My glory," says the Lord (Isa.43:7). It pleased the Lord Jesus to put His glory upon His Church in the world. No other group has been chosen by God except His redeemed children to display His glory. The Church, therefore, is the only entity given the responsibility and privilege of displaying the glory of God in a tainted world. And it does so in the corporate worship and prayer. No one will mar His glory. "And before all the people I must be glorified," says the Lord (Lev.10:3). Listen to the words of Isaiah: "And My glory I will not give to another" (42:8), because none is able to reflect His glory. God said through the prophet Ezekiel: "I will set My glory among the nations" (39:21). The future of the true church is translation and glory (1Thes.4:14-17). Our Lord Jesus Who is the very expression of God and the radiance of His glory (Heb.1:3), just before His Crucifixion gave the glory of God to His Church. (John 17:4, 5, 6, 10, 22). Therefore, we are to display the glory of God in corporate worship.

However, the symbolism is not complete if the Church reflects only the glory of God. The Church comprises imperfect human beings who have fallen into sin, but are redeemed by the blood of the Lord Jesus. And when man's fallen glory is present in the Church, which is not a perfect entity, reflecting the glory of God alone would not be the correct position for it. The Church must also reflect its true character, the fallen but redeemed glory of humanity.

Man, according to verse 7, is the glory of God, but the woman is not the glory of God; she is the glory of man. In other words, woman was made to manifest man's authority and man's will as man was made to manifest God's authority. Hence, the woman is the vice regent who carries out man's wish, as man is the vice regent who carries out God's wish. Therefore, women are to submit, and men are to be in authority in the church. That's why, Paul says in I Corinthians 14:35, "And if they want to learn something, let them ask their own husbands at home."

In Genesis 1:26-27, we read, "And God said, 'Let Us make man in Our image, according to Our likeness; let them have dominion over the fish of the sea, over the birds of the air, and over the cattle, over all the earth and over every creeping thing that creeps on the earth. So God created man in His own image; in the image of God He created him; male and female He created them.'"

God created man to rule over, and therefore He gave him dominion over, everything in the universe. Throughout history, men have ruled the world in all the areas of life. Men have been the ones in authority because God originally endowed it within them.

God does not have a physical image and, when man was originally created, he was created in the moral and intellectual image of God. As a result, he was created with free will, emotion, righteousness, and true holiness. Because of the fall, man's glory is marred, and it is restored when he comes back to Christ. "And that you put on the new man which was created according to God, in true righteousness and holiness." (Eph.4:24). The plan of God was not just to redeem the people from their sins, but to restore His image to their lives. It is the fulfillment of the prophetic words of the Lord Jesus: "Though I have stolen nothing, I still must restore it." (Psalms 69:4).

When Adam was created, Eve was in Adam. To be a helper to man, woman was created from the rib bone of man. God says that He created man in His image, and He created them male and female. So He also made woman equally in the image of God, in every aspect, and that image is restored in Christ. A woman will be just as much like Jesus Christ when we see Him face-to-face as a man will be.

As John MacArthur says, "Even though a woman is in the image of God, a woman is not the glory of God. She is not the outshining of God, but she is the outshining of man, because she is derived from man. So, man can be compared to the sun, and woman to the moon. She shines not so much with the direct light of God, but that derived from man."

God's glory is far superior to man's glory and cannot be compared with anything in this universe. Therefore, Paul says, "that no flesh should glory in His presence" (1:29). "He who glories, let him glory in the LORD" (1:31). "Therefore let no one boast in men" (3:21). The reason is that because the woman is the glory of the man, and man's glory is the fallen glory. Therefore, the woman must have her head covered to symbolize this fallen glory. "If there had been no fall, there would not have been the need for woman's head covering," says Peter Wee, "but because of the fall, man's glory is marred, and this is shown in the woman's head being covered. As both Adam and Eve sinned, the fall involved both man and woman. Therefore, the head covering of the woman symbolizes the fallen glory of both, man and woman."

When a woman covers her head, it is not the sign of her submission to man, or merely an ancient Corinthian custom, but it speaks of an important doctrine—that of the fallen glory of man and woman who have been redeemed. If the woman's head is exposed, it assumes a status equal to the glory of God, but woman is the glory of man. Therefore, man's glory must be placed in proper perspective, completely outshined by God's glory. In the church gatherings, the head covering of the woman conveys man's fallen glory. Indeed, it represents the fallen glory of both man and woman, as both have sinned and have been redeemed. At the same time, the uncovered heads of man properly reveal God's glory. Thus, both man and woman fulfill their respective roles of manifesting glory.

When we come together for worship, angels are observing and they are pleased when the whole assembly reflects the unveiled glory of God in its radiance, as symbolized by man's unveiled head, and the fallen glory but redeemed of mankind, as represented by woman's veiled head. Woman is the helper to man in his responsibilities and she is the steward of the head covering.

"One's dress reflects the principles that one lives by; even our exterior must conform to the order that God has established, especially in matters pertaining to communal worship," explains Dr. Sproul. "The apostle makes the point that the veil as a symbol of authority is inconsistent with the position of man, but it is required for women who are subordinate to man" (Coram Deo, "Head Covering Is Required for Women" 18 June 1996).

One might ask, "Why must woman reflect man's glory? Can't both she and he reflect God's glory?" Paul answers that question by going back to the Creation order. "For man is not from woman, but woman from man. Nor was man created for the woman, but woman for the man." (1Cor.11:8-9). When Solomon says, "An excellent wife is the crown of her husband" (Prov.12:4), the meaning is that she is made for her husband.

Paul says that whenever Christians come together, women are to follow the etiquette of submission and men of headship. When a woman wears head covering in the assembly, she is affirming her role of submission, acknowledging that man is the glory of God and she is the glory of man (v.7). But in this age of feminism, when women refuse to accept their God-ordained roles in the church and family, they undermine the foundational design of God, and the purpose for which woman was made.

Culture and Worship

Some people think that uncovered women in the first century were throwing off Greco-Roman standards and that they fell into two groups: Feminists and those engaged in immoral activities. But this may not be true. From the wealth of literary, statuary, and visual representations (frescos and other paintings in homes, temples, and public squares), it is clear that Greco-Roman culture did not generally expect a covering on women. On the other hand, Oriental culture did, and this culture includes the Jews, whose women were recognizable in North Africa in the second century because of their veiling in public.

Paul says that if a woman refuses to cover her head in the church, she would rather shave her head like the women who did so because they wanted to become like men (v.4). Shaving her head to look like man was a reproach to woman at that time. In the Old Testament times, shaving the head of a man or a woman was embarrassing (Deut.21:11-14; Ezra 9:3; Neh.13:25; Isa.3:24; 50:6; Jer.7:29; Ezek.5; Micah 1:16; 2Sam.10:4).

When Paul delivered the principle to the Corinthians, and to the rest of the Churches (v. 16), he was introducing a practice strikingly counter-cultural to Greco-Roman and Judaic traditions. The Corinthian women had not been flouting their own culture; they had been following it, in opposition to Paul's teachings.

"Nowhere does [Paul] give cultural reasons for his teaching, i.e., abusive practices of a pagan society that placed prostitutes with shorn heads in the temples," says Dr. Sproul. "Paul points us back to God's established order in nature. Whenever a teaching in scripture refers to 'creation ordinances,' that teaching is binding for all cultures in all ages" (Coram Deo, "The Head Covering Command Is Binding Upon All Cultures," 20 June 1996).

There is no suggestion in Paul's words that cultural factors in Corinth motivated him to instruct women to cover their heads. Nor there is any indication that this commandment is intended solely for Corinthians in their cultural setting. Paul says that the reasons for head covering lie rooted in the way God created man and woman. The head covering is a sign of the subjection of not only woman, but all mankind (vs. 3-4, 7-10).

While the head covering symbolizes submissiveness and obedience, we should never think that the outward sign alone conveys spirituality nor that its absence indicates carnality.

Overall, there are five main reasons for head covering:

◆ Based on the principle of headship (1Cor.11:2-5)

◆ God's order in relation to creation (1Cor.11:6-12)

◆ Because of angels (1Cor.11:10)

◆ Based upon what nature itself teaches (1Cor.11:13-15)

◆ Instruction of Paul from his apostolic authority (1Cor.11:16)

■

Chapter 9

The Equality of Men and Women in Light of the Bible

The Bible teaches that both man and woman were created in God's image, had a direct relationship with God, and were heirs to all blessings (Gen.1:26-28). As God's redeemed children, men and women are equal before Him, but they have different roles. Spiritually speaking, women and men are not only equal (Gal.3:28), but women are to be treated with respect and honor as the weaker partner and heirs of the gracious gift of life (1 Peter 3:7).

As Adam and Eve were co-participants in the fall (Gen.3:6; Rom.5:12-21; 1Cor.15:21-22), Jesus Christ came to redeem all mankind, women as well as men. Through faith, we become one in Christ, and heirs to every spiritual blessing in Christ Jesus regardless of gender (John 1:12-13; Rom.8:14-17; 2Cor.5:17; Gal.3:26-28). Spiritually speaking, all believers are chosen to be part of the holy priesthood and to offer spiritual sacrifices acceptable to God through Jesus Christ (1 Pet.2:5, 9; Rev. 1:6, 5:10). All are representatives of God to the world (2Cor.5:20).

Headship and Subjection: The Trinity

While all Three Persons—God the Father, God the Son, and God the Holy Spirit—are of the same in essence in the Godhead, there must be headship and subordination to maintain order. In the Holy Trinity, God the Father precedes God the Son, and God the Son precedes God the Holy Spirit, yet all are consubstantial and co-eternal. Though the Son is subordinate to the Father and the Holy Spirit to the Son, all are equal in Trinity. Lord Jesus is the head of the man in the relationship between our Lord Jesus and humanity and man is subordinate to the Lord Jesus.

In the beginning, man was created before woman. Since the woman comes after the man in the creation order, she is subordinate to the man; therefore, man is the head of the woman and woman is subordinate to man in the relationship within mankind. Matthew Henry observes that woman was not created from man in order to dominate him, but to be a co-equal, to stand under his arm for protection and near his heart for love.

Even before the fall, God gave headship to man. "The man was to be responsible and accountable to God, the woman to be his helper and supporter." (*Focus on the Head-covering*, Ritchie Booklets No.9). Positionally, Eve was equal to Adam, but Adam was the head and was responsible for her actions. Although Eve sinned first, it is by Adam, the head, that sin is said to have entered the world. Paul speaks repeatedly of the one man, Adam, who brought sin and death into the world (Rom.5:12-21). Since Adam is the head of the human race, he bears responsibility for the fall, even though Eve sinned first. As a descendant of Adam, Eve's sin brought death to her only, but Adam's sin caused death to every human who derived from him. When Eve took over the God-given authority of Adam and communicated with the enemy independently, she was deceived. That fact strengthens the truth that women were designed to need a leader.

In 1 Corinthians 11:3, Paul is saying that Christ is the authority over every man, man is the authority over woman, and God is the authority over Christ. Since Paul appeals to dominance among members of the Holy Trinity, it is clear that he does not view the relations described here as merely cultural.

In 1 Corinthians 11:7-10, Paul writes about women's submission in connection with the creation. Therefore, it is not a custom and this injunction is applicable for all times. Man's headship and woman's subjection were God's order in creation. Although man and woman were given dominion over all the creations, the headship was given to man. While woman is the glory of man and man is the glory of God, He has made man His representative to rule over. The uncovered head of man is the silent witness of this fact. Woman is not made as a head like man, but she is the glory of man.

The Meaning of "Man and "Woman"

In Greek, *aner* means "man" and *gune* "woman." However, some translators have rendered these terms as "husband" and "wife," implying that only husbands' heads should be uncovered and wives' heads covered. Unmarried men and women remain untouched by Paul's injunction. When we examine the reasons for head covering, we see that this interpretation cannot be correct. All people—married and unmarried—come under the commandment. Hence the proper translations of *aner* and *gune* are clearly "man" and "woman."

Since head covering reveals the condition of the heart, it will make sense only when the heart aligns with it. Therefore, a woman should not wear the veil on her head until she is wearing it first on her heart. There is no sense in covering her head unless she is in subjection. The most important element is the proper state within. A woman who wears the veil on her heart accepts the place that God gives to women in the Church, in the family, and in the society. Head covering is a symbolic of humility, submissiveness and obedience. Verses 7-10 of 1Corinthians 11 deal with the submission of the woman to man in relation to the creation order, and Paul concludes that covering the head is not a custom at that time.

Subordination

In the creation account, it is indisputable that Adam was created first, and then Eve; hence man precedes woman and woman is subordinate to man. However, this subordination does not mean that woman should take orders from man like a military officer. Apart from creation order, man and woman are the same.

It is God who designed, initiated, and established the marriage relationship for mankind (Gen.2:23-24). Therefore God has given the husband authority over the wife in the marital relationship.

1. Subordination Does Not Mean Subjection

Let's look at the difference between subordination and subjection. According to the sequence of creation and design of God, wives are subordinate to their husbands, and this relationship is especially proper for an orderly management at home. A wife is subject only to her own husband—not to any other man.

There is no injunction in the Scripture for an unmarried woman to be in subjection to any man except to her father. A woman's authority is transferred only by marriage (from father to husband), as mentioned in Numbers 30:3-16. Subjection of wife to husband is only within the family, and the husband is not to dominate his wife or force her to be submissive to him, but to love her. Indeed, there should be mutual submission between husband and wife (Eph.5:21-33; Col.3:18, 19; 1Pet.3:1, 5-6). Here we are not considering the family order of wifely submission to the husband, but the creation order of subordination of woman to man in the assembly and in other spiritual gatherings.

Subjection does not imply subjugation by force, but submission by choice. "Obedience can be forced, but submission is evidence of a yielded heart," says Warren Henderson. "God did not create the woman for man to wipe his feet upon nor was she created to rule over him."

Subordination doesn't make one inferior. Submitting to divine roles does not degrade women or exalt men, but rather it glorifies God. Christ took the form of a servant and lived a life that was pleasing to His Father in perfect obedience. Christ was not inferior to the Father during His earthly ministry of subjection. Just as Christ's subjection to the Father does not imply His inferiority, differences in role do not logically imply inferiority or inequality.

To redeem mankind, Christ chose to submit Himself in all things to the will of the Father, and He is a perfect example for all Christian women. In fact we are called to follow His example. H.G. Mackay says, "In accepting the place of subjection to the headship of the man, Christian women have the high honor of emulating the Son of God. And in doing so, they demonstrate to angelic observers the restoration of the divine order of headship which had been violated by the self-assertion of Lucifer, and the disobedience of Adam and Eve" (Assembly distinctives).

Anyone who rejects the idea that women are to be submissive to men must also reject the facts that church is to be submissive to Christ and that Christ was submissive to the Father in His incarnation. The relationship is clear in 1 Corinthians 11:3: "But I want you to know that the head of every man is Christ, the head of woman is man, and the head of Christ is God."

Christian women must follow the example of Christ who emptied himself and became obedient unto death on the cross in order to redeem the mankind, the radiance of God's glory and the exact representation of His being, who sustains all things by His powerful Word.

2. Subordination Does Not Mean Inferiority

Dr. Peter Wee adds that "there is nothing to indicate that man is superior to woman anatomically, physiologically, psychologically, academically, socially, morally or spiritually. There is no basis for comparison. Both are different, each complements the other, and neither is complete without the other; at the same time both are interdependent. What one lacks the other supplies. Under such circumstances, no superiority in nature can be claimed by man although man is ahead of woman in position and authority before God in creation. God has made man the leader, the one who makes decisions generally."

Therefore, woman's subordination to man does not mean she is inferior or in subjugation to man, to be ruled as a servant, slave, or possession. "Who, being in the form of God, did not consider it robbery to be equal with God, but made Himself of no reputation, taking the form of a bondservant, and coming in the likeness of men" (Phil.2:6-7). As the Christ is subordinate to the Father, yet equal to Him and of the same essence of the Godhead, woman is subordinate to man, yet is equal to him and of the same human essence. Subordination does not mean inferiority, but it is the splendor of a divine order.

Women are not below men in terms of essence, personality, thinking, or anything other than the role assigned. In the same way, many employees are not in any way inferior to the boss, and some may be more intelligent. All the superiors have is a different role, or a position to assign work to the subordinates.

Hence there is equality, but a difference in the assignments God has given to man and woman. Authority cannot function without submission, and submission cannot function without authority. They are mutually dependent.

In the church we have elders and deacons. Elders are not spiritually superior to deacons, although some elders are interested in taking the authority over them. There is a spiritual equality among the believers, but they have different responsibilities. Jesus Christ said, "But you, do not be called 'Rabbi'; for One is your Teacher, the Christ, and you are all brethren" (Matt.23:8). The Apostles support this equality: "Yes, all of you be submissive to one another, and be clothed with humility" (1Pet.5:5); "Submitting to one another in the fear of God" (Eph.5:21). The same is true with a man and a woman. Just because the husband is the head of the house doesn't mean that he is in any sense superior and the wife is inferior in essence or in personality. He simply has a different role.

3. Equality and Interdependence

Because woman is man's subordinate, some might say, "Certainly this teaches that woman is inferior to man and is subject to him." Apostle Paul refutes this argument: "Nevertheless, neither is man independent of woman, nor woman independent of man, in the Lord. For as woman came from man, even so man also comes through woman; but all things are from God" (v.11-12).

Here, Apostle Paul says that both woman and man are fused in the Lord. Then he makes it clear that although in creation woman came from man, in procreation every man is born of woman (v.12). Therefore, without woman, there would be no man on planet earth, and without the first man Adam, there would be no woman on earth. That is the balance and there is equality in procreation as women give birth to men. There is a difference in roles, but a beautiful equality in the Lord.

God saw that it was not good for Adam to be alone (Gen.2:18). Just as man is not complete without woman, church is not complete without women. In Christ, male and female are equal and we find the truth of sublime reciprocity here. "There is neither Jew nor Greek, there is neither slave nor free, there is neither male nor female; for you are all one in Christ Jesus" (Gal.3:28). All things are of God. God is the creator of mankind and He is the one who is responsible for our existence and survival on earth. Therefore, men and women are equal. Neither is inferior to the other, but rather they complement each other. Moreover, they both should glorify God and thus fulfill the purpose for which they are created.

The man is not inferior to Christ, his head, because God sees the man in Christ, and Christ is certainly not inferior to God. He is God. There is a difference in role assignment. Likewise, the woman is not inferior to the man.

Therefore, Paul says, there is a principle of authority and submission here, but it is based on love, not tyranny. The Father loved the Son and the Son loved the Father. Christ loves the church and the church loves Christ. In the same manner, the husband loves the wife and the wife loves the husband. Authority and submission merge through love.

1 Corinthians 11:9 says, "Nor was man created for the woman, but woman for the man." God did not create man from the woman or for the woman. Rather, woman came out of man; she was from man and was made to help man. "Nevertheless, neither is man independent of woman, nor woman independent of man, in the Lord" (v.11).

Here Paul is referring to the church in the Lord. The meaning is that, in the church, men depend on women as much as women depend on men. The church plainly needs the participation of women. In fact, if the women do not carry out their role, men cannot either. In many churches, women do most of the basic work.

In the Old Testament, the law was given for men and women. God appeared to both, and both served God. When we come to the New Testament, both men and women again serve the Lord. Both are responsible for all the commandments. They are warned about all the curses and are given all the promises. In terms of spiritual life and blessing, all are equal. Both men and women have the same spiritual responsibility before God to live to His glory. On the spiritual level, we are all equal and yet we have different roles. Therefore, in Old and New Testaments, there is equality of spiritual life but not of role.

In the Lord, women are exalted to the place of men (Gal.3:28). Peter says that a husband and a wife are heirs together of the grace of life (1Pet.3:7). They are equally dependent on each other. Spiritually, they are a resource to one another. Women always had a vital part in the life of the first-century church. There were widows who ministered to the saints, washed their feet, gave them food and housing, taught the children, blessed their own husbands, and carried out the role of helpers or deaconesses.

There is a beautiful equality that makes man dependent on woman as woman is dependent on man in the Lord. Mutually, in the body of Christ, we all work together for His glory as the body is rooted, built up, and edified. Nobody can say men do not need women. Men cannot be independent. They are incomplete without women. So there is obviously a place of equality for women in the Christian church, in Christ.

Neither is the man without the woman and the woman without the man in the Lord. "For as woman came from man, even so man also comes through woman; but all things are from God" (1Cor.11:12). As woman came out of Adam, man comes out of Eve, but note that "all things from God." In other words, God created man and woman. Every man and woman is a loving gift of God. Women and men are divine creations.

The beauty of this comes out in 1 Timothy 2:15, where Paul says, "Nevertheless she will be saved in childbearing if they continue in faith, love, and holiness, with self-control." Some think this passage means that a Christian mother will be saved from death in the physical act of childbearing. Others think childbearing refers to the birth of the Messiah, and that women are saved through the One (Christ) who was born of a woman. The most reasonable interpretation is that although no public ministry in the church is assigned to woman, she in fact does have an important ministry. God has placed her in home and more specifically in the ministry of raising children for the honor and glory of the Lord. In other words, every man born into the world has to come from a mother. She may be submissive to a man, but women are the ones who, for the most part, shape the men.

"The thought is that if the husband and wife maintain a consistent Christian testimony, honor Christ in the home, and raise their children in the fear and admonition of the Lord, then the woman's position will be saved," says William MacDonald. "But if the parents live careless, worldly lives, and neglect the training of their children, then these children may be lost to Christ and the church. In such a case, the woman does not achieve the true dignity which God has ordained for her."

Lilley states, "She shall be saved from the results of sin and be enabled to maintain a position of influence in the Church by accepting her natural destination as a wife and mother provided this surrender is further ratified by bringing forth the fruit of sanctified Christian character."

That's how God harmonizes and balances the roles. John MacArthur says, "If the women in Women's Liberation really wanted to change the world to the way they like it, they ought to go home and raise their children in the fear of the Lord. The woman is saved in child bearing. That's the greatest and richest calling and honor that she bears, and it's all of God."

4. Creation and Procreation

Marriage and procreation were God's design for man, but God in His infinite wisdom, gave man relational capacities and a helper suitable for him. "And the LORD God said, "It is not good that man should be alone; I will make him a helper comparable to him" (Gen.2:18). The term "helper" doesn't mean somebody to cook, take out the trash, make the bed, wash the plates, or change children's napkins. God provided a helper for man in the propagation of the human race.

Genesis 1:27 say "male and female He created them and 5:2 say "He created them male and female, and blessed them and called them Mankind in the day they were created." God created man first and named him Adam. God looked all around His creation and there was no partner for Adam in all the created order. He needed a perfect match out of the ground the Lord God had formed. Therefore, we see something different about the way he formed this helper (vv. 21-24). "And the LORD God caused a deep sleep to fall on Adam, and he slept; and He took one of his ribs, and closed up the flesh in its place. Then the rib which the LORD God had taken from man He made into a woman, and He brought her to the man. And Adam said: 'This is now bone of my bones and flesh of my flesh; She shall be called Woman, because she was taken out of Man.'" (Gen.2:23).

The man is not of the woman, but the woman is of the man. Man did not come from woman, but woman came from man. Woman was made from man for man. So Eve was made from Adam for Adam, and then she was brought to Adam. John MacArthur says, "The origin of woman, her reason for being, and Adam named her 'Eve' is God's clear statement that man is in authority, and she is in submission." Therefore, man is not to wear the symbol of submission.

Here's how God created man: In the beginning, God made them male and female. "In the image of God He created him; male and female He created them" (Gen.1:27); "And the LORD God formed man of the dust of the ground" (Gen.2:7). Verse 2:7 is not an additional story, but an expansion on the original. Genesis 1:27 and 2:7 tell us that God created the man first, and 2:22 says He created the woman following. In both verses, the male is first.

Bible scholars say that the book of Genesis is amazingly accurate. Genetic research confirms that the male has both an X-chromosome, which procreates females, and a Y-chromosome, which procreates males; however, females have only two X-chromosomes. If the woman had been created first and the man was fashioned from her bone, only females could have been reproduced, for there would be only X-chromosomes. The Y-chromosome is necessary for males; therefore man had to be created first because he has both an X- and a Y-chromosome.

The Omniscient God created man first and programmed the DNA in the cell structure so that it could produce a male offspring. Then He fashioned a woman partner out of Adam and together they could produce both male and female. Therefore, God encoded both the X-chromosomes and Y-chromosomes, even though it is not explained in the book of Genesis. The male had the DNA such that a female could be taken out of him and be genetically related to him in the same kind, and through her he would be able to procreate both male and female. Thus, together they fulfill the mandate of verse 28: "Be fruitful and multiply and subdue the earth."

God made two genders and He designed each one for a specific purpose. When we study the male and female anatomy, it becomes evident that we were wonderfully fashioned to "fit" together. This is not only true in a sexual context, but psychologically as well. Eve, being suited to Adam's particular needs, was given to him as a "help-mate." Man and woman were divinely created to complement each other.

Chapter 10

Liberation of Women

The Women's Liberation Movement in America was formed to promote gender equality and establish equal rights and legal protection for women. There are political, cultural, and sociological hypotheses, as well as philosophies, concerned with issues of gender difference in feminism.

At the time of Christ, in the Roman and the Greek world, women were thought of as purely slaves and animals. It was Jesus Christ who elevated their value in the society by showing them compassion and respect in a way they had never known. Schreiner says, "Jesus treated women with dignity and respect and he elevated them in a world where they were often mistreated."

Yet Jesus did not exalt women to a place of leadership over men. This fact demonstrated their equality in every dimension except in the assignment of role. It therefore helped women and men see their God-ordained design and fulfill it with a commitment. The greatest proponent of the liberation of women was not the National Organization of Women (NOW). It was the Gospel of Jesus Christ that gave meaning to life.

The Roman culture brought cultural abuses to women, but they sometimes reacted with abuses of their own. As John MacArthur states, "What apparently happened in Corinth was sort of an abuse of Christian liberty. Some of the women, feeling that they were free in Christ, began to throw away their veils. For example, women were maintaining their independence in those days by refusing to have children, or if they had children, they refused to take care of them. They demanded jobs always held by men, by wearing men's clothes and discarding all signs of femininity." If we study the history, it is crystal clear that the feminism of ancient Rome is similar to the feminism today. In fact, it had all of the characteristics of feminist movements at all times in history.

Charles Erdmann points out another interesting parallel in the Corinthian situation: Some women in the Corinthian and Roman society were uttering statements against the sacredness of marriage. There was a feminist movement even on a broader base in the Roman Empire, and women often would take their veils off and cut their hair. They sheared their hair to look like men and they flung away the veil to protest the inequality of men and women, and these were all visible signs of their antagonism toward the sanctity of marriage. In my opinion, today the Women's Liberation Movement is similarly liberating women from marriage and motherhood.

Jerome Carcopino was a historian who chronicled the history of the Roman Empire, focusing on Corinth around the time of the New Testament. In his words, "Women were running around bare breasted with spears in their hands stabbing pigs and climbing poles trying to get equal rights with men" (*Daily Life in Ancient Rome*).

When Christianity arrived and declared equality of women in spirit and personhood, this event liberated them from bondage and feminist attitudes have carried into the church too. As John MacArthur says, "The women's liberation movement has found its way into the church and now we have Christian feminists who are advocating the fact that there is only in Christ equality. They wave the flag of Galatians 3:28, that in Christ there is neither male nor female. On this basis, and on the basis of 1 Peter 3:7, that a husband and a wife are heirs together of the grace of life, they postulate the fact that there is no such thing as authority and submission between men and women, either in marriage, in the church, in business, in education, or in any other dimension."

Wherever the gospel has spread, the status of women—socially, legally, and spiritually—has risen. Women converted from pagan religions to Christianity were freed from humiliating practices and they rose to prominence in home, in church, and in society where they were honored and admired for feminine qualities like caring their families, showing hospitality, reaching out to the needy, and ministering to the sick. Wherever the gospel has been obscured (whether by oppression, false religion, or spiritual suppression within the church), the status of women has fallen accordingly.

Men and Women Are Not Alike – A Biological View

We discussed the chromosomal contrast between man and woman earlier. But they are only the start of our overall biological differences. Even a quick examination of them can give us a greater appreciation for the unique and wonderful way we are made. Below are some of them:

- ❖ Women have three key bodily functions absent in men: menstruation, pregnancy, and lactation. Each has a major impact on their lives.
- ❖ The sexes have different shapes, in ways few people notice consciously. Women have a smaller head, broader face, softer chin, shorter legs, and longer trunk.
- ❖ Women live longer. In the United States their lifespan is typically three or four years greater than men's, and a similar pattern prevails everywhere.
- ❖ Women have a lower basal metabolism rate than men.
- ❖ Emotionally, females respond faster and more fully than men. They cry and laugh more easily.
- ❖ Relatively speaking, women have a larger liver, stomach, kidneys, and appendix, but smaller lungs. Indeed, women's lungs have only 70 percent of men's capacity.

- In women the first finger is typically longer than the middle one; with men the middle finger is longer.
- Men's teeth are more durable overall than women's.
- Female hormonal patterns are more varied and complicated. The glands work differently in the two sexes. For example, a woman's thyroid is bigger and more active, and plays a role in the smooth skin, relatively hairless body, and thin layer of fat under the skin that add to her beauty. Her thyroid also enlarges during menstruation and pregnancy, making her more vulnerable to goiter.
- Women's blood has only 80 percent as many red cells as men's. Since these cells bear oxygen to the body, women tire faster and faint more easily.
- Men have 50 percent greater muscle strength.
- Women's hearts beat more rapidly (80 vs. 72 beats per minute on average). Their blood pressure averages ten points lower than men's and varies more from minute to minute. However, they have less tendency to high blood pressure—at least among women who have not yet experienced menopause.

God authored those differences and we should appreciate them. In fact, they bring great freshness and vitality to our lives. How boring it would be if the sexes were identical! How redundant it would have been for the Creator to put Adam to sleep and then fashion yet another man from his rib!

God brought forth a woman and gave her to Adam. He put greater toughness and aggressiveness in the man, and more softness and nurturance in the woman—and suited them to each another's needs. And in their relationship, He symbolized the mystical bond between the believer and Christ Himself. What an incredible concept! We need to celebrate our differences. (Adapted from Dr. James Dobson, *Love for a Lifetime*, Multnomah Gifts, 2003).

■

Chapter 11

The Multi-Level Spiritual Truths in the Head Covering

The spiritual truth of head covering is emphasized by Apostle Paul in 1 Corinthians Chapter 11: "But I want you to know that the head of every man is Christ, the head of woman *is* man, and the head of Christ *is* God" (1Cor.11:3).

This verse makes it clear that male headship is a permanent and God-ordained arrangement. It is not a cultural phenomenon. Paul highlights three headship-subordination relationships: Christ-man, man-woman, God-Christ. The head of Christ is God and we are to follow the headship of Christ in submission (Eph.5:23-33; 1Pet.3:7). Note that Christ, God, and man are each called a head. Only woman isn't.

Let's look at the three headship relationships closely.

1. The Head of Every Man Is Christ

"The head of every man is Christ" (1Cor.11:3); "For man is not from woman, but woman from man" (1Cor.11:8). God made man first and gave him dominion and then created woman to be his helper. The man is not from the woman, the woman is from the man (11:8-9).

God could have created man and woman simultaneously, but He

didn't. Adam alone was created directly by God and he in no way derived from a woman. "And the LORD God formed man of the dust of the ground, and breathed into his nostrils the breath of life; and man became a living being" (Gen.2:7). That is the beginning. Then we read: "And the LORD God said, 'It is not good that man should be alone; I will make him a helper comparable to him.' Out of the ground the LORD God formed every beast of the field and every bird of the air, and brought them to Adam to see what he would call them. And whatever Adam called each living creature, that was its name. So Adam gave names to all cattle, to the birds of the air, and to every beast of the field. But for Adam there was not found a helper comparable to him. And the LORD God caused a deep sleep to fall on Adam, and he slept; and He took one of his ribs, and closed up the flesh in its place. Then the rib which the LORD God had taken from man He made into a woman, and He brought her to the man. And Adam said: This is now bone of my bones and flesh of my flesh; she shall be called 'Woman', because she was taken out of Man." (Gen.2:18-23).

When Timothy says, "For Adam was formed first, then Eve" (1Tim.2:13), that is not cultural. When we ask, "Who came first, the man or the woman?" we are not asking about the priority of the chicken or the egg. As verse 8 says, woman was made from man for man. The origin of woman and her reason for being born is God's clear statement that man is in authority, and she is in submission. Again, this is not a natural, intellectual, functional, or spiritual inferiority, but simply the different roles designed by God for His greatest creation, man and woman.

Therefore, in all spiritual gatherings, at home, in church, and while women pray, women need to cover their heads. Since Christ the Son is the head of the man, and the God the Father is the head of Christ, why do we debate about whether the man is the head of the woman?

2. The Head of Every Woman Is Man

Paul makes it clear: "Head of the woman *is* man" (v.3), "But every woman who prays or prophesies with her head uncovered dishonors her head" (v.5). He is emphasizing that since man is the head of the woman, when a woman prays, she ought to have her head covered. Head covering is needed not only during worship, but also at prayer meetings and any spiritual gatherings.

In light of these verses, a woman who does not submit to the God-given authority of man dishonors her head, the man. However, when a woman subordinates herself and obeys the injunction of God by covering her head, and a man represents Christ in authority, it is the visible manifestation of bride submitting to the bridegroom.

J.B. Nicholson Sr. says, "Verse 3 sets the foundation for the lesson in headship. It teaches the divine order of authority."

In 11th Chapter, there are three symbols: the head, the bread, and the wine. The head represents our relationship in the spiritual Body; the bread and wine speaks silently of the sacrifice of His physical body. As we do not have the freedom of omitting any of these three symbols, how the 'Head' can become insignificant?

It is also significant that even in 1 Corinthians 11:3—"The head of every man is Christ: and the head of the woman *is* the man; and the head of Christ *is* God"—the Spirit of God does not put the woman first, though it would otherwise be logical in the rising scale of authority.

This verse says nothing about inferiority. The clause "the head of Christ *is* God" stands directly parallel to the clause "the head of the woman *is* the man." However, since Christ is God, He is not inferior to God the Father, just as in alphabetical order, the letter 'A' is no more important than any other letter. Similarly God has established order in the world and in the church. "Let all things be done decently and in order" (1Cor.14:40).

Apostle Paul states that as Christ is the head of every man, any man praying or prophesying (teaching) with a covered head is dishonoring his head, which is Christ (1Cor.11:4). Christ must not be dishonored.

Prophecy is the proclamation of God's truth in the language of the people. It has two aspects: revelation (when prophet spoke), and reiteration (when we teach from the Bible).

While man's head is uncovered, the woman is asked to cover her head. "But every woman who prays or prophesies with her head uncovered dishonors her head" (v.5). By the uncovered head, the woman dishonors her figurative head. As man is the image and glory of God, he does not need to cover his head. "Since he is the image and glory of God; but woman is the glory of man" (v.7). In the light of these verses, when a man covers his head or any woman uncovers her head, it is contrary to the teaching of headship.

3. The Head of Christ Is God

Finally, we come to: "The head of Christ *is* God" (v.:3). The two important doctrinal truths in this verse are: Christ is the head of every man and salvation demands submission to this head. It also reveals the fact that if a person is not a born-again believer in Christ, he will never acknowledge the Lord Jesus as the head of creation, head of the church, and head of the family.

· Therefore, head covering also incorporates the doctrine of salvation. A redeemed man or woman will willingly and joyfully recognize and admit His headship, and obey the commands of the Head. Since head covering has to do with headship—the headship of Jesus Christ—the saved one would be properly submissive to obey His command. By covering the head in a spiritual gathering, a woman declares to the world that she has been redeemed by the Lord and respects Him as head of the Church and head of man. So whoever follows the correct head-covering practices (bare head for men and covered head for women) acknowledges Christ's authority, command, and redemptive work on the cross.

■

Chapter 12

The Woman's Personal Glory: A Double Covering?

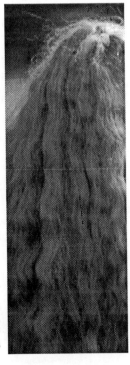

In 1 Corinthians 11:14-15, Apostle Paul illuminates the personal glory of woman: "Does not even nature itself teach you that if a man has long hair, it is a dishonor to him? But if a woman has long hair, it is a glory to her; for *her* hair is given to her for a covering." Why God has given long hair as a covering for a woman? Here, he stresses that long hair is vital to her because it is an expression of her personal glory. This covering is given to all women, saved and unsaved alike, but it is a privilege and responsibility for a Christian woman to wear additional covering.

Double Covering

In verse 15, Paul writes that a woman's "hair is given to her for a covering." If so, why does he also state in verse 6 that "she should be covered" with a piece of fabric? On the surface, it seems unnecessary and Paul's statements appear contradictory. Hence some critics hold that since women already have one covering, they do not need another. However, that interpretation contravenes the text. We have to note that two coverings are mentioned in this passage and there is an analogy in verse 15 between natural and the spiritual.

William MacDonald puts it this way: "The actual argument in verse 15 is that there is a real analogy between the spiritual and the natural. God gave woman a natural covering of glory in a way He did not give to man. There is a spiritual significance to this. It teaches that when a woman prays to God, she should wear a covering on her head. What is true in the natural sphere should be true in the spiritual."

"The natural long hair of a women is God's natural covering to go around the head and face," says William Kelly, "and that beautiful natural 'covering' is to be covered of hidden by another covering during preaching and praying."

Kelly and J.N. Darby both construe the end of verse 15 to mean "given her instead of a veil," that is, instead of a covering she would otherwise wear constantly as a frame for her head and face. It is her natural covering and it stands apart from what she adds to her head during prayer and preaching.

Some critics say that men have beautiful long hair too. Even if it is true, for man to wear the glory of woman is a paradox in the sight of God and of the angels.

There are two views about the covering.

View 1

Paul mentions that long hair is given her for her personal glory. It is a glory "to her." While the woman represents the glory of the man and the woman, the woman's individual glory resides in her long hair, given to her for her own covering. Therefore, every Christian woman has a dual role to fulfill in the congregational prayer and worship: Her long hair is a glory and a covering for her, and the head covering she wears symbolizes the fallen glory of both man and woman.

View 2

Women's own fallen glory is symbolized by her long hair which is both her glory and her covering. The Greek word for "veil," *peribolaion*, differs from that for head covering, *kata kephales echon*. *Peri* in *peribolaion* means "around," and *ballo* means "throw like a mantle." The distinction between woman and man is the veil she wears, and the distinction between her and man is the long hair given her for a covering, which is the figurative veil.

Dr. Sproul says, "It is obvious from this comparison between men having their head uncovered and women having their heads covered, that the covering is not hair. For if the covering in this context were hair, verse 6 would make no sense in the context of this passage" (*Coram Deo*, "The Women's Hair Does Not Qualify As the Head Covering," 18 June 1996).

"It is only in the past century," says John Peter Bodner, "that some commentators have attempted to make this 'hair equals head covering' argument. Whether we look at Hebrew women in the Old Testament, or Christian women through the ages (and in a variety of different cultures), God's people have always understood that the head covering is a piece of cloth or clothing worn upon head and not merely a woman's long hair."

John Wesley observes, "If she will throw off the badge of subjection, let her appear with her hair cut like a man's.... But if it be shameful for a woman to appear thus in public, especially in a religious assembly, let her, for the same reason, keep on her veil."

There is also an inherent difference in the meaning conveyed by the two coverings. Long hair comes automatically from nature, but a woman voluntarily puts on the head covering in church, and hence she is showing her obedience to God. In Jamieson, Fausset, and Brown's *Commentary*, we read: "As woman's hair is given by nature as her covering (v.15) to cut it off like a man would be palpably indecorous; therefore, to put away the head-covering like a man would be similarly indecorous. It is natural to her to have long hair for her covering: she ought, therefore, to add the other head-covering, to show that she does of her own will that which nature teaches she ought to do, in token of her subjection to man."

Dr. Sunny Ezhumattoor makes the difference clear: "God's glory is to be seen alone in the assembly of the saints. In order to do this, the man's head remains uncovered by not having long hair and by removing any head covering, because the man is the image and glory of God (I Corinthians 11:7). Any covering on the man would veil God's glory. Women, however, are the stewards of their coverings. There are two competing glories in the church. 'The woman is the glory of man' (I Corinthians 11:7) and 'If a woman have long hair, it is a glory to her' (I Corinthians 11:15). Because there are two symbolic glories to be covered, there must be two coverings. The first head covering, Greek (*peribolaion*), is the woman's long hair (verse 15) to hide the glory of the man (the woman herself). The second head covering, Greek (*katakalupto*), is to hide her glory, which is her own hair. In this way, God's authority is declared in the church. By it, the men are reminded that, in their ministry, their glory is to be hidden. The angels are also instructed by it (I Corinthians 11:10)." (A Brief Outline of the "Plymouth Brethren": History, Doctrines, and Practices)

Darby on Head Covering

J.N. Darby says, "Observe here the way in which the apostle grounded his replies with regard to details on the highest and fundamental principles. The subject is a direction for women. They were not to pray without having their heads covered. To decide this question, simply of what was decent and becoming, the apostle lays upon us relationship and the order of the relationship subsisting between the depositories of God's glory and Himself, and brings in the angels to whom Christians, as a spectacle set before them, should present that of order according to the mind of God. Then he adds that the man was not created for the woman, but the woman for the man. Their relationship with other intelligent creatures that were aware of the order of the ways of God included that their heads were to be covered. This was necessary because the angels were spectators of the ways of God in the dispensation of redemption, and of the effect this marvelous intervention was to produce. However, man was not to cover his head, because he represented authority. In this respect he was invested, as to his position with the glory of God, of whom he was the image. The woman was to have her head covered as a token that she was subject to the man, her covering being a token of the power to which she was subject. Man however could not do without woman, nor woman without man. Finally, the apostle Paul appeals to the order of creation according to which a woman's hair, her glory and ornament, revealed in contrast with the hair of man that she was not made to present herself with the boldness of man before all. Her hair served as a veil, and portrayed modesty, and submission, which was her true position, and her distinctive glory." (*Synopsis of the Books of the Bible*)

In the Old Testament, Kohathites were delegated to cover the tabernacle and the utensils (Num.4:4-15). In the same manner, the sisters in the New Testament have been assigned with the office of the coverings in the church. In the presence of God, women should make sure that all glories that are competing to the glory of God are covered and concealed. In order to display the glory of God, even the cherubim and seraphim use their wings to cover their own inherent glories in heaven. The same example is given to us in the church. God will not tolerate any competing glories in His presence. For example, Lucifer was lifted up because of his beauty; he corrupted the wisdom by reason of his brightness. "You were the anointed cherub who covers; I established you." "By the abundance of your trading You became filled with violence within, and you sinned; therefore I cast you as a profane thing out of the mountain of God; and I destroyed you, O covering cherub, from the midst of the fiery stones" (Ezek.28:14, 16).

As Warren Henderson observes, "The sisters, like the Kohathites of old, have been entrusted with the ministry of the coverings within the house of God. They are to cover and conceal all glories that compete with God's glory."

A 17-year-old girl was asked why she wore a head covering. She replied, "Even if I don't fully understand everything about it, I would cover my head as my hair is my glory. But why should my glory be seen when I desire that Christ's glory be seen?" ∎

Chapter 13

What Does Nature Teach?

Nature as well as the Bible is unambiguous about the distinctions between men's and women's hair. "Does not even nature itself teach you that if a man has long hair, it is a dishonor to him? But if a woman has long hair, it is a glory to her" (1Cor.11:14). This verse states clearly that long hair is a glory for woman but an offense for man in the eyes of God and of the angels.

The shame of long hair in man is evident in nature. But God ordained that a Nazarite, one separated to Him, grow hair until the vow had been completed. It is clearly a hardship: "Speak to the children of Israel, and say to them: 'When either a man or woman consecrates an offering to take the vow of a Nazirite, to separate himself to the LORD, he shall separate himself from wine and similar drink; he shall drink neither vinegar made from wine nor vinegar made from similar drink; neither shall he drink any grape juice, nor eat fresh grapes or raisins. All the days of his separation he shall eat nothing that is produced by the grapevine, from seed to skin. All the days of the vow of his separation no razor shall come upon his head; until the days are fulfilled for which he separated himself to the LORD, he shall be holy. Then he shall let the locks of the hair of his head grow'" (Num.6:2-5).

By the law of the Nazarite, one must endure the reproach of nature and other people while he finds joy, peace, and satisfaction only in God. We see the perfect fulfillment in our Lord Jesus Christ. The Bible is silent about the length of His hair, even though many people think that the Jesus Christ had long hair, as seen in paintings. Contrary to modern artists' conceptions, there is no reason to believe He actually did have long hair. Jesus is the Word, and His written Word says that it is a shame for a man to have long hair. From the drawings and sculptures of men during the time of Jesus' earthly ministry, it is evident that men did not generally have long hair.

Some male philosophers and men in pagan tribes did have long hair, even down to their shoulders. However, wherever men had long hair, women had longer hair. The distinction is always clear and visible. Therefore, we cannot say these men were rebelling against God. Paul is very plain about hair: men's and women's should be distinct. There's no reason to blur the line. This does not mean that everybody is to have short hair or long hair, but rather that we should make a conscious effort to seem as we are.

Despite what many people assume, the fashion of men growing hair did not come from the Beatles or modern trends. In Revelation 9:7-8, a mass of locusts arose from the bottomless pit. "Their faces were like men's faces; they had hair like women's hair." Perhaps it is the idea of Satan to make men look like women. While God wants us to be in the likeness of his divine nature, Satan tries hard to destroy the natural order of man and woman whom God has created.

With the formation of the New Testament Church, we received clear instructions about how to maintain the distinction between man and woman. Therefore, we must comply with the Word of God and put it into practice. We are not to conform to the pattern of this world, but be transformed by the renewing of the mind (Rom.12:2).

The Physiological Difference

Paul observes that nature itself teaches us to pursue God's plan to lead a pleasing life in His sight. For example, the Creator has organized the human anatomy in such a way that it explicitly unveils the truth that men are to have short hair and women long hair.

We should never think that people with long hair are spiritual and those with short hair are not. Long hair doesn't make anyone holy. Anyone can grow long hair, so hair length cannot measure anyone's spirituality and spirituality cannot be a justification for growing long hair. The point is that nature gives men shorter hair than women.

This fact is physiologically true. A scientist named Ken Anderson researched the matter and proved that hair grows in a three-phase cycle. First comes the formation and growth of new hair. Next, the hair ceases growth and rests. Third, it becomes loose and ultimately falls out. Then the cycle starts all over again.

The male hormone testosterone speeds those three stages, so that man gets to the third stage faster and the hair falls out. That is why we see a lot of bald men but virtually no bald women. Aristotle said, "I have never seen a bald child, eunuch, or a woman." (Today, we mainly see them as a result of human interventions such as chemotherapy.) The reason is that testosterone speeds up the steps to reach the third stage quickly, and that limits growth in a man.

The female hormone estrogen causes the first cycle, the growing stage, and prolongs in woman longer than in a man. That is why a woman's hair will grow longer than a man's before it falls out.

Paul is saying: Isn't nature teaching you something? Hasn't God revealed the truth in physiology that short hair belongs to men and long hair belongs to women?

Nature and Instinct

In Greek, the word for nature is *phoosis*. But we can also translate it as "instinct." Instinct means the instinctive, "natural" sense of man as he interprets what he sees in society. If we look around us, it is clear that men have shorter hair than women. Nature has taught and man has agreed with nature. In all history, around the world, men have generally had shorter hair than women.

As mentioned before, some men in the past centuries did have long hair, even to the shoulder, but the women's hair was down around the top of the legs. In ancient Rome, long hair was considered part of women's identity and Roman writers ridiculed it among men. Early church councils condemned men with long hair as well. The Bible says that men are to have shorter hair than women. God has given long hair to women by nature and to men short hair that he might manifest the divine authority of God. God designed the distinction into human nature and human instinct.

The apostle concludes his instructions to the Corinthian church by saying that women in all churches have head covering. "But if anyone seems to be contentious, we have no such custom, nor do the churches of God" (1Cor.11:16). That is, if any of you want to argue against it and be "contentious," then "we have no such custom, nor do the churches of God."

Note that "churches" in the above verse is plural. The Church in Corinth was instructed to adopt the practice prevailing throughout the Christian churches at the time. The apostles and the churches universally agreed about the meaning of God's command. If anybody wished to argue, the complaint should go to God, not to Christians who obey His command.

Archeologists have found sculptures, etchings, and carvings of people in the early church, particularly in the catacombs. In every case, men have short hair, and the women have long hair, and their heads were covered while praying. That was the undeniable custom in the early church. It was universal and it should always be universal according to the Word of God.

■

Chapter 14

Practical Aspects: Who, What, and When?

We have so far been considering the doctrinal aspects of head covering. Now let us look at the practical applications, such as who is to wear what kind of head covering on which occasions.

Kind of Head Covering

Since head covering is a symbol of the fallen glory of both man and woman, it should be simple: a piece of fabric to cover the head. Many women use a lace scarf. Some argue that the whole face must be covered, but there is no justification for this practice. In Islam, for social reasons, women in some countries use veils to cover the face completely. The purposes of these veils are different from that of Christian worship, where the head signifies glory and the face is of no importance. A veil to cover the face is unscriptural because the symbolism requires only a covering for the head. Besides, the true veil of the woman is her long hair, given her as a covering (1Cor.11:15).

Who Should Wear One?

All women who have believed in Christ and identified with His death, burial, and resurrection through water baptism should cover their heads, because the word *gune* refers to "woman" and not "wife." Whether they are teenagers or adults, single or married, married to believers or unbelievers, they should don a head covering as long as they have believed and been baptized. No female believer is exempt from the injunction of Holy Spirit.

At What Age Should a Woman Start Wearing One?

She can wear it from the age she is born again. But it is good to practice head covering earlier. "Bring them up in the training and admonition of the Lord" (Eph.6:4).

In fact, even girls can wear the covering. Dr. Peter Wee states, "Since woman came from man before the fall, man reflects the glory of God and woman, the glory of man, and this glory may be displayed even through little boys and girls. As glory can be manifested by all men, women, boys and girls, in relation to creation rather than redemption, parents can encourage their little daughters to have a head covering and their little sons to remove their hats at assembly gatherings even prior to their salvation. Some assemblies carry this practice and it is highly commendable."

Oversight

The church is the pillar and the foundation of truth (1Tim.3:15). Therefore the oversight should encourage the sisters to observe the command of the Lord when they gather for prayer and worship, as they are the protector of the God's household. If one of them refuses to obey the Lord's command and persists in ignorance, there should be no compulsion (1Cor.14:38), but rather the devout should pray for them and commit the matter to the Lord.

Born-Again Men

Every man who has believed in the Lord Jesus must uncover his head in worship and prayer. Jewish men pray with a prayer shawl, or *tallith*, covering the head (top, sides, and the back). Roman men did the same. Arab men wear a *keffiyeh* (*guthra*) on their heads (top, sides, and back) to keep out dust in desert areas and protect them from harsh weather conditions. All such head coverings are to be put aside. Whoever he is and whatever his situation, the man must remove his head covering so the glory of God can stand revealed when His people come together for worship.

Conclusion

It is the Son who revealed God the Father to us. "No man has seen God at any time, the only begotten Son, who is in the bosom of the Father, he has declared (revealed) *Him*" (John 1:18). The glory of God is completely revealed in the Lord Jesus Christ. The Church will continue to reveal the glory of God until the second coming of Jesus Christ as God's glory has never diminished. Therefore, we have to reveal His glory as we come to worship.

Man reflects the glory of God as he is created first and he is the glory of God, while woman reflects the fallen glory of man and woman. But both are equal in the sight of the Lord and interdependent because while woman came from man, every man comes by woman through birth. While men worship with uncovered heads, the full glory of God is manifested and signified, and when women worship with covering on their heads, the fallen glory of both man and woman is signified. This is practiced in gatherings of God's people for worship and prayer, conferences, and in certain circumstances (such as Sunday school and sisters meetings) where women also teach. By submission, women do not become inferior or men become superior, but instead only God receives the glory. If we disregard the practice of displaying the glory of God as different from the glory of man, we are in danger of violating the injunction of the Lord (Eph.3:21).

■

Chapter 15

The New Practice

Paul anticipates possible counter-arguments about head covering, especially the appeal to precedent: "No one did it before the Christian Church arose. Why should we practice it now?"

Establishing the Practice

Paul's answer is: "we have no such custom, nor do the churches of God" (1Cor.11:16). The meaning is that it was indeed not in practice earlier. The New Testament Church was formed only after the events of the resurrection and Pentecost. After the completion of salvation of mankind and with the formation of New Testament Church, when God's glory is revealed, this practice became necessary to display God's glory and man's fallen glory. There was no such custom earlier in the Greco-Roman or Jewish circles, but now it is indispensable in the gathering of saints. In fact, Paul is asserting that, apart from this practice, there is no other manner by which the glory of God can be displayed in the church.

In William Kelly's opinion, Paul is saying that women praying or prophesying without head covering in God's church is not courteous.

Paul warned men against covering their heads, though they had done so in earlier customs. When Paul asked women to cover their heads, it was not based on a cultural background, but the practice is associated with, and is an expression of, the following doctrines:

- ◆ The authority of the Lord
- ◆ The inspiration of the Holy Spirit
- ◆ The authority of His Word
- ◆ Revelation by the Lord
- ◆ Headship and its meanings with regard to salvation
- ◆ Submission to the Lord, and subordination to man
- ◆ The glory of God
- ◆ The image and glory of man
- ◆ The glory of woman
- ◆ The fact of creation
- ◆ The equality and interdependence of man and woman
- ◆ Because of angels
- ◆ Obedience to the Lord's commands

The observance of head covering in the spiritual gatherings is the external manifestation of a believer's willingness in the realm of submission and obedience to Christ. Therefore, it should be observed with joy and gratitude. Neglecting and ignoring the practice is disobeying the command of Christ and rejecting New Testament truths.

Chapter 16

Beyond the Head: Appearance, Spirit, and Apparel

How should godly women dress in our modern world? To address this question, we must start back in the first century.

Dress and Fashion in the Greco-Roman World

The most basic garment in Roman clothing was the "tunic" (*tunica*), the standard dress of the day. The male tunic generally reached nearly to the knees, while the female version was longer, and sometimes touched the ground. Men in ancient Greece customarily wore a "chiton" similar to the one worn by women, but knee-length or shorter.

As the Archeological Bible says, "In the Greco-Roman world clothing basically fit into two categories: the tunic and the mantle. The tunic was something like the modern T-shirt, but very long (of knee length or angle length). A mantle was rather like a large blanket wrapped around a person.

"The tunic (or chiton) was the basic article of clothing for virtually all people. Lower class women often wore only an ankle-length tunic, gathered by a belt across the upper abdomen, while women of higher economic status added a mantle—often either a himation or a peplos over the tunic. The himation for women was smaller than that for men. But the patterns and coloring, as well as the size, did distinguish whether a himation was intended for a man or a woman."

The Appearance of a Godly Woman

Man and women should dress differently from each other because it is a natural upshot of creation. Women have to maintain the conventional femininity that God has made in them. The Bible has a few guidelines to a godly woman's dress code. Deuteronomy 22:5 deals with this issue. "A woman shall not wear anything that pertains to a man, nor shall a man put on a woman's garment, for all who do so are an abomination to the LORD your God."

The verse refers to more than clothing when it says that woman shall not wear that which pertains to man. It refers to anything that belongs to man that would tend to change roles. A person wearing the clothes of the opposite sex is called a "transvestite." This is a sexual fantasy problem, and according to some statistics, as many as one out of ten people have it.

Some people think it is a sin for a woman to wear pants because Deuteronomy 22:5 says that a woman should never wear "that which pertains to a man." However, at that time men didn't wear pants; instead they wore tunics. Therefore pants did not belong to either gender and that statement doesn't make any sense at all, but today it is very difficult to recognize the God-designed distinction between man and woman. John MacArthur says that "textually we can't make a case against women wearing pants, but anything that tends to obliterate the distinction, God frowns on seriously."

The implied meaning of this verse (Deut.22:5) is that people should never alter their appearance to look like the opposite sex. It may also be saying that the woman should appear in the role consistent with her femininity according to the culture, and the man similarly in a role consistent with his masculinity, and there should never be a willful merging of those.

However, in modern culture, men and women wear confusing outfits that can make it hard to recognize gender by apparel. The term is "unisex." This is part of satanic work. There are unisex stores where we can go in and buy all kinds of things that look the same for both genders. Maybe this is the idea of Women's Liberation Movement, which attempts to make a woman look like a man to wipe out any obvious distinction. The truth is that a man should look like a man and a woman should look like a woman. Women have to make every effort to look like a woman in their dress. It's very important for them to appear feminine, and that is the essence of Deuteronomy 22:5.

The picture above appears all around the world. It is a universal symbol, and it shows the basic distinction between man and woman: Men wear pants and women wear skirts. Imagine the confusion if both men and women were portrayed in pants. Apostle Paul, inspired by the Holy Spirit, went to great lengths to show that there has to be a difference between men and women, and for good reason.

Does a Christian Woman Dress Differently in the World?

Scripture gives a clear mandate with regard to female dress. Women need to be modest and not extremely stylish.

What dress qualifies as modest? In essence, it is complete, simple, and inexpensive. John Chrysostom defined it as garb that "covers [women] completely and decently, and not with superfluous ornaments; for the one is decent and the other is not. What? Do you approach God to pray with braided hair and ornaments of gold? Are you come to a ball? A marriage-feast? A carnival? There such costly things might have been seasonable: here not one of them is wanted. You have come to pray, to ask pardon for your sins, to plead for your offences, beseeching the Lord…. Away with such hypocrisy!"

William MacDonald adds, "First Timothy 2:9 forbids expensive clothes: It is not a matter of whether we can afford it or not, but it is sin for a Christian to spend money on expensive clothes because God's Word forbids it. Compassion forbids it too."

Yet modern fashions are not designed to encourage spirituality. Although we are subject to our times, we should never adopt all the immodest fashions. We can wear any kind of dress we want to, unless we claim to be godly. God designed clothing to cover, not to draw attention to, the sexuality of both men and women (Gen. 3:21; Lev. 18).

"One of the functions of clothing is to hide man's nakedness. At least, that's the way it was in the beginning, but now clothing seems to be designed to reveal increasingly large areas of the anatomy," states William MacDonald.

Melody Green says, "Measure the time we spend for dressing and maintain an equal time for God. 'Redeeming the time, because the days are evil' (Eph. 5:16). Many people go to the other extreme by being untidy, uncaring about themselves. This is self-righteous. God needs a balance. To married couples, she says, there's nothing wrong in dressing to please your partner, but not at the expense of others."

Since God is holy, we need to go to God's presence in respectful apparel. "Oh, worship the LORD in the beauty of holiness!" (Psalms 96:9). The RSV's "holy array" takes this as the beauty of the priests' holy garments in worship. "The mention of holy garments reminds us that even the clothes we wear when we worship the Lord should be appropriate to the occasion," says MacDonald. As we are the bride and we are given the robe of righteousness, when we come to God's presence, we need to put on the clothes that give due glory to his name.

The Israelites had to wear clothes according to Old Testament law. "Speak to the children of Israel: Tell them to make tassels on the corners of their garments throughout their generations, and to put a blue thread in the tassels of the corners. And you shall have the tassel, that you may look upon it and remember all the commandments of the LORD and do them, and that you may not follow the harlotry to which your own heart and your own eyes are inclined and that you may remember and do all My commands, and be holy for your God" (Num. 15:37-39).

Therefore, in ancient times all Jews wore such tassels on the corners of their upper garments (that is, upon the four corners of the himation), as a reminder to themselves that they were God's people and lived under His law. Our Lord Jesus Christ also wore the garments according to the Law. It is written that a woman who had an issue of blood for 12 years came behind him and touched the hem of his garment (Matt.9:20).

The Pharisees

The Pharisees were motivated mainly by a craving for the praise of men, as a public show "to be seen" by others (Matt.6:1). "But all their works they do to be seen by men. They make their phylacteries broad and enlarge the borders of their garments" (Matt.23:5). It was a showy, superficial display of their religion. John MacArthur says, "A Pharisee's broad phylacteries and the jumbo-sized tassels on the four corners of his robe (cf. Deuteronomy 22:12) were fitting metaphors for the many ways the Pharisees made their religiosity as ostentatious as possible. They were almost constitutionally incapable of doing any act of charity or piety without making a tawdry public display out of it in the process. Because Pharisee-style religion is motivated mainly by a craving for the praise of men, it is inherently self-aggrandizing, making it the very antithesis of authentic charity."

As Matthew Henry explains further, "The Jews were distinguished from their neighbors in their dress, as well as in their diet, and thus taught not to be conformed to the way of the heathen in other things. They proclaimed themselves Jews wherever they were, as not ashamed of God and his law. The Jews were commanded to make tassels on the corners of their garments and to put a blue thread in the tassels of the corners. Blue is the heavenly color, and it was intended to speak to them of the holiness and obedience which suited them as children of God.

"The fringes were not appointed for trimming and adorning their clothes, but to stir up their minds by way of remembrance, 2 Peter 3:1. If they were tempted to sin, the fringe would warn them not to break God's commandments. We should use every means of refreshing our memories with the truths and precepts of God's Word, to strengthen and quicken our obedience, and arm our minds against temptation. Be holy unto your God; cleansed from sin, and sincerely devoted to his service; and that great reason for all the commandments is again and again repeated, I am the Lord your God. Our Savior, being made under the law, wore these fringes; hence we read of the hem or border, of his garment (Matt. ix. 20)."

There is no virtue in shabbiness and untidiness. Oswald Chambers says, "Slovenliness is an insult to the Holy Spirit. The believer's clothes should be clean, pressed, in good repair, and well-fitting."

"Jeans and slacks are much more comfortable at work," says Elizabeth Elliot, "if riding on a horse back or doing athletic activities. But skirts are in one way much more comfortable. We need not to be dressed up. Dress is a matter of respect. We are subject to our times and therefore should not adopt all the fashions. It is the principle that we have to follow."

Modesty After the Apple

After Adam and Eve had sinned, when they knew they were naked, they tried to cover their nakedness with the leaves of the fig tree. Then God gave them a better, safer leather garment, in a picture of divine providence and redemption. He thereby taught us the fundamental truth of worship and the basic principles of dressing even in the earliest stage of mankind. Thus we have to bear in mind that man cannot stand naked in the presence of God.

As Matthew Henry says, "This teaches us modesty and decency of garb and gesture at all times, especially in public worship, in which a veil is becoming. It also intimates what our souls need have of a covering, when we come before God that the shame of their nakedness may not appear."

Early in the morning, Jesus Christ appeared to his disciples in His resurrected body by the Sea of Tiberias. Hearing that it was the Lord, Peter wrapped his outer garment around him (for he had taken it off) and jumped into the water (John 21:7). While fishing, it was a normal practice for the fishermen to wear only the inner garment and roll the outer garment on their heads. Another time, when Peter saw the Lord and remembered about His holiness, he fell at Jesus' knees and said, "Depart from me, for I am a sinful man, O Lord!" (Luke 5:8).

Zechariah saw Joshua, the high priest, standing before the angel of the Lord, and Satan standing at his right side to accuse him, as Joshua was dressed in filthy clothes. The Lord rebuked Satan, and the angel said to those who were standing before him, "Take away the filthy garments from him." Then he said to Joshua that he would put rich robes on him. (Zech.3:1-4). These passages teach us that in the presence of God and because of angels, we need to be in modest attire.

Similarly, God gave instructions to Aaron and his sons who were separated for the priesthood that they should make linen undergarments as a covering for the body, reaching from the waist to the thigh. "And you shall make for them linen trousers to cover their nakedness; they shall reach from the waist to the thighs. They shall be on Aaron and on his sons when they come into the tabernacle of meeting, or when they come near the altar to minister in the holy place, that they do not incur iniquity and die" (Exod.28:42). In the original tongue the same word is used here as for the garments of skin God made for Adam and Eve in the garden when they felt their nakedness.

Should Women Wear Skirts?

The question of whether women should wear skirts has spurred considerable discussion. One side of the argument states that since our body types are more or less the same and pants are more convenient, why not let the women wear them? Most critics say that the intention of women to wear pants is to signify that they are equal with men. So let us look at the origins of women wearing pants.

The first attempt by the feminists to put their ideals into the practice was through the bloomer. This outfit included a skirt reaching halfway between the knee and the ankle. Beneath the skirt, Turkish trousers came down to the ankle where an elastic band gathered them tight. Although Elizabeth Smith Miller introduced this outfit, Amelia Bloomer popularized it and her name became attached to it. However, the bloomer was short-lived. These "unsexed" women, as they were called, provoked a great controversy — so great, in fact, that the feminists finally abandoned the bloomer. At the same time, the Civil War focused all attention on the plight of the nation. As a result, the move for dress reform and women's emancipation faded away.

Nevertheless, these issues reappeared during the last quarter of the century, though the arguments were still the same. Feminists claimed that skirts and other womanly apparel were the garb of female slaves, worn solely to please male masters, and that only more "reasonable" dress could free them to enjoy equal vigor and competition with men. Gradually, they moved toward it.

At first, women wore men's clothes only at home, but it was not long before women in pants appeared in industrial work, in outdoor activities, and on the streets. For instance, the Wigan pit brow girls scandalized British society by wearing trousers to work in the coal mines. They wore skirts too, but rolled them up to the waist. In the 19th century West, women on ranches donned pants to ride horseback.

In the early 20th century, aviatrices and other working women often wore trousers. By the 1920s, women were openly embracing styles like pants and short skirts for the first time. Designers made dresses fit close to the body to emphasize elegant trimness. Actresses Marlene Dietrich and Katharine Hepburn were often photographed in pants and helped make them acceptable for women. During World War II, many women took on jobs previously held by men and sometimes wore pants, and in the 1950s they became acceptable for gardening, the beach, and other leisure activities.

By the 1960s and 1970s, a vast array of clothing had become popular, including miniskirts, hot pants, and blue jeans. In the 1960s, André Courrèges introduced long trousers for women as a fashion item, and by the 1970s pants were common. In 1972, the U.S. Congress passed Title IX of the Education Amendments, which mandated equal treatment of males and females in public education. As a result, schools could not require dresses of girls.

Today, women often wear pantsuits and designer jeans, and indeed they wear pants far more often than skirts. Bans against them wearing pants in the workplace and fine restaurants have almost vanished. Many women wear them almost all the time. (Pendergast, "The History of 20th Century Women's Clothing," 2004, http://www/randomhistory.com)

These are certain principles for dressing and they apply to both men and women:

1. Modesty. Does this clothing cover me adequately? (1Tim.2:9)

2. Avoidance of worldliness. Does it simply reflect the current trends of Hollywood and TV? (1John2:15)

3. Difference. Does it easily show there's a difference between me and the opposite gender? (Deut.22:5)

4. Inoffensiveness. Does this clothing offend a brother or sister in Christ? As a woman, will this cause my brother to stumble or think lustfully about me? (Rom.14:12-13; 1Cor. 8:13; 10:24)

5. Glory to God. Does it glorify God, or does it highlight and glorify me? (1Cor.10:31)

Below is a letter sent to Elizabeth Elliot from a distressed young man who sought her answer to a prevalent matter that illustrates the scarcity of sound biblical teaching, whose provision is the duty of older Christian women.

Dear Mrs. Elliot,

I am a youth leader at a church. You came to speak at our church. Remember the dinner with the youth leaders at [so-and-so's] residence? I am writing today with a concern. Lately, I have been noticing how the girls in our group are dressed. There's no cleavage showing, but the skirts are short. Some of the blouses are sleeveless and a couple of the shirts are a little too tight.

They're fashionably dressed, and if I may use the term, tastefully sexy. By now I hope you're getting the picture. Incidentally, the women who dress in this way include the ones which I would consider spiritually maturing. Well, we guys are having problems dealing with lust. Our main youth leader, a single man, did address the issue once in a girls' only meeting.

To sum up the talk in one statement, he informed them that when women dress in any way which arouses the guys, they no longer appear as individuals but as objects. He encouraged them to be modest dressers. The talk was good, in that many of the girls were not aware of what goes on in guys' minds when a tastefully sexy woman walks by.

I know it would have been more appropriate to have a woman speak on this subject; unfortunately, we have no strong, mature female leader. Perhaps the Lord will send one someday, one who will end up marrying the youth pastor. Two months have gone by since the talk and there has been no change in the dress code. One of the comments I've picked up by a girl was, "Why should the weakness of the guys force us to change the way we dress? It seems to be a lack of self-control on the part of the men."

Elizabeth, what should the youth leadership do? Should we enforce a dress code? Should we send women home if they come to church with sleeveless blouses or skirts above the knee? How do we set a standard? Should we just pray and do nothing else? We're already praying about the situation. Is there a book you've written or a discussion on tape or a video on the subject, which you would recommend? What should the guys do in the meantime besides stop staring?

Basically, I'm writing for advice because I trust your point of view. You and Lars are two of my mentors. Not all of your admirers are women, I'm sure you know. I'm a 24-year-old man who has read most of your books. My Redeemer saved me six years ago. My desire is to have the same attitude and zeal for Christ as Jim Elliot, Amy Carmichael and Betty Scott Stamm had. I will appreciate your comments."

Here's a letter from another man:

Why do Christian women dress to expose themselves? I am very bothered by this. I believe that you are the one for me to tell. I hope I won't be crude, but I think that I will have to be frank to completely express myself. Why do the women dress to expose themselves? Even in church I have seen them wearing dress that have at least one slit that goes almost all the way up to the crotch, see-through blouses and no slip and low-cut blouses. They don't want to be treated like sex objects, but then they dress like prostitutes. I can understand why secular women dress that way, but I can't understand why Christian women do. I can't understand how anyone could. Do I have a problem? Would you please address this issue some time?

Let's look at the reply from Elizabeth Elliot:

What does modesty mean? Well, it means placing a low estimate on one's own merits, not being forward or showing off. It means unpretentious. Modesty means to be free from undue familiarity, from indecency, from lewdness, pure in thought and conduct. Speaking of modest apparel, it means decent, seemly. The opposite of modesty is conceit, boldness, immodesty, brazenness, lewdness.

Let's think first what immodesty says about us women before we talk about what its effects may be upon others. What are your Christian standards? Do you seek to be noticed, to make a splash when you come into a room? Or do you seek to be simple, humble, gentle and quiet in spirit and not wearing the very latest fashions nor looking frumpy by wearing something that's way out of date. We do have to conform to a certain degree, but there're always classic clothes. Those are the ones that I try to stick with because they last for many years. I have a suit now that I think is 17 years old and I just wore it about a week ago. I wear things which are tailored and simple and classic. My principles that I'm articulating go back about 2,000 years.

But we're talking about these low-cut dresses, sleeveless blouses, see-through blouses and the slit skirts. Does a man's thought life have a problem? Well, of course. As both of these men recognized, it is their job to stop looking. Don't look the women up and down. Don't fall for the types who are dressing like prostitutes. But is it right for us women to be thoughtless in these areas? Is there earnestness about pleasing the Lord? Have we taken His yoke? Are we learning from Him? Are we gentle and humble in heart? Are we walking worthy of the Lord, looking and acting and speaking differently from the world?

The Bible says that we're supposed to shine as lights in the world. Christ lives in me. Does that make any visible differences? Will it correct my thinking? Do I pray that God will purify my desires? Prostitutes dress obviously, so as to draw attention. It's their business, isn't it? The last thing that a Christian woman is thinking of is being like a prostitute. But here is some very frank talk from two different men in two different places, and it's not by any means the only letters that I've had from them. It is a very difficult and a very delicate question.

What would the Lord have you do? Look like a frump or look like the vanguard of the fashion magazines? Flashy or sober? Are you pregnant? Are you overweight? Do you try to dress in such a way as to minimize those things? Are you too old for short skirts? I see a lot of women as I travel around who I would certainly say are too old to be wearing those short skirts. And if you're 16 years old, how short a skirt can you wear if you want to be responsible before God in the presence of young men? Neat or messy? Wildly and deliberately messy? I see some hair-dos which I think of as wildly and deliberately messy. Feminine? There are many ways of drawing attention to yourself without your once thinking about it. Think. Ask the Lord's guidance. We older women must be willing to take the risk of making someone angry and speaking to her about the way she is dressing. We have to take responsibility. It is our fault that we have not been teaching younger women modesty.

Although I cannot control what other people wear, especially on the outside world, it seems disrespectful to me to see ladies in church in very short skirts or skimpy, sleeveless tops. I would imagine that it could be distracting to men who are trying to keep their minds on God. We need voices like yours, "A voice of one crying in the wilderness."

Here's one letter from a woman:

I wanted to comment on your subject today about modesty and older women teaching younger women. I, too, am bothered by those who come to church inappropriately dressed. Although I cannot control what other people wear, especially on the outside world, it seems disrespectful to me to see ladies in church in very short skirts or skimpy, sleeveless tops. I would imagine it could be distracting to men who are trying to keep their minds on God.

And in fact, it is distracting to women like me, who instead of concentrating on the message or the worship, are sitting there thinking about how inappropriately the others are dressed. I think that one should dress with modesty and respect when they are coming into the house of the Lord. My mother used to tell me that Jesus is the King of kings and if you were going to visit the king or queen, you would certainly try to look your best. So you should do no less when you're going to God's house. I think she was right, and I try to convey that same attitude to my two small daughters.

I also wanted to comment on the issue of older women teaching the younger women. You suggested that there are not enough older women who are willing and available to teach and advise younger women in the church. We don't have enough of them in ours. While I do appreciate the friendship and advice of older women who have grown children, I also think that all of us should think of ourselves as potentially being the older woman. I do not think the older women must be seniors to fill this role.

Elizabeth Elliot says, "It is our fault that we are not teaching younger women modesty." Older women are to teach the younger women (Titus 2:3-5). Yet where are these older women? Many do not bother.

Men have a responsibility not to let themselves have lustful thoughts. Women have a great responsibility not to provoke them. "Let nothing be done through selfish ambition or conceit" (Phil.2:3). Women must ask themselves if they are dressing out of mere conceit. "Do not merely look out for your own personal interests, but also for the interests of others" (Phil.2:4). Women must ask if they are just being selfish. Christian women need to be aware of the male thought pattern and dress carefully. As she says, "We should have a searchlight on our hearts and motives for the way we choose to dress."

While speaking in a conference where 95% of the audience members were gray-haired women in slacks, Elizabeth Elliot said, "Slacks are not distinctively feminine dress for a woman and I do not recommend women to wear shorts or slacks. Many use short skirts, clothes too tight, tops that are cut too low due to lack of concern and responsibility as a representative of Jesus Christ. Shorts and slacks are not the most feminine apparel to choose unless it is necessary working in the garden, horse riding, shoveling snow etc. Try to be womanly and not manly."

Referring to Deuteronomy 22:5, she says, "There always was some distinction between women's and men's dress, although men were not wearing pants [in the first century] and both men and women wore ankle length robes. There was always some indication. But inch by inch a woman's ankles, calves, upper arm, etc. once concealed began to be visible in the 20th century. These were regarded as threats to the society's stability. Failure to recognize the God-given glorious inequalities—distinctions between masculine and feminine—will result in God's judgment. We have a responsibility before God to be feminine, self-controlled and pure so that nobody speaks of evil about us (Titus 2:3-5). Look at the mirror and check for transparency. Don't major in sweat pants and sweat shirts."

Melody Green says, "God does not think beauty is evil. How could it be? He invented it in the first place, but beauty corrupted becomes harlotry." She quotes from Ezekiel 16: "How many of you are acting like harlots, parading yourselves, seducing with your eyes and trusting in your looks to bring you love and acceptance instead of trusting in God and putting your confidence in Him." It is said that "beauty is only skin deep," and that is true. But God sees through the inside, and the things that are beautiful to Him are not apparent to the common eye. The world teaches us that to be loved we must be beautiful, sensual, and alluring. We are assaulted daily by billboards, books, TV programs, magazines that teach us a different gospel. "True beauty is Jesus and Him alone. Letting that love flow through us to others, is the beauty that is pleasing to God. True beauty radiates from the face of godly men and women; you won't notice much what they really look like because you are too busy noticing Jesus in them. Should not that be our goal? Let us allow Jesus to fully indwell in us that we would never do anything that will bring shame to His name, yielding our whole life to Him, serving him in the inner courts of his blessedness. Let's not forget that we are his bride and dress accordingly as we fully devote ourselves from the world and clothe ourselves with the righteousness of God."

Thus, instead of buying costly raiment, the author of *Believer's Bible Commentary*, William MacDonald, purchased clothes from Goodwill stores.

According to *Character First*, "After her husband died, Margaret Haughery became a laundress at the upscale St. Charles Hotel in New Orleans. But she could see the poor out her window, and she decided to do what she could to help them. With her meager savings, Haughery bought two cows and sold milk from door to door. Before long, she started giving her hard-earned money to charities and orphanages.

"Haughery eventually opened a bakery and started distributing bread to orphanages and charities for free or at a reduced price. Haughery eventually helped establish eleven orphanages and several homes for the elderly.

"Despite her success, Haughery owned only two dresses—one to wear during the week and one for Sundays and holidays. When Margaret died in 1882, she left $600,000 to charity." (*Character First*, 4th Edition Bulletin No.7)

Our bodies are precious because they are a gift from God and created in His image. They are attractive, because we are made by God. Therefore God doesn't want our bodies exposed in an unworthy manner. Apostle Paul says, "Present your bodies a living sacrifice, holy, acceptable to God" (Rom.12:1), "Walk worthy of the calling with which you were called" (Eph.4:1), "Walk worthy of God who calls you" (1Thess.2:12), and "You may walk worthy of the Lord, fully pleasing *Him*" (Col.1:10).

During the reign of Uzziah people enjoyed great prosperity and as a result, the women embraced an unpleasant materialism (Isa.3). Their manner of walking and dressing reflected the condition of their heart. Isaiah describes how women strolled through Jerusalem: "Because the daughters of Zion are haughty, and walk with outstretched necks and wanton eyes, walking and mincing as they go, making a jingling with their feet" (3:16). Look at the phrases "walking and mincing as they go" and "making a jingling with their feet." Mincing is a sort of sexual walk, one adopted to attract attention. They made a tinkling because they wore bells on their feet. Thus, these women were clearly putting on a show to allure men and entice their attention.

In Isaiah 3:18-23, God pronounces judgment on them: "In that day the Lord will take away the finery: The jingling anklets, the scarves, and the crescents; The pendants, the bracelets, and the veils; The headdresses, the leg ornaments, and the headbands; The perfume boxes, the charms, and the rings; The nose jewels, the festal apparel, and the mantles; The outer garments, the purses, and the mirrors; The fine linen, the turbans, and the robes." God will remove forever 21 things used as adornment to seduce men. Women who are haughty and lustful, and who call attention to themselves for their own evil purpose, will be judged.

Isaiah 3:17 is a condemnation of Israel's women. "Therefore the Lord will strike with a scab The crown of the head of the daughters of Zion, And the LORD will uncover their secret parts." Because the daughters of Zion are haughty, God was angry to the point of judgment. In verse 8, He says, "Jerusalem is ruined, Judah is fallen," and in verse 11, "Woe to the wicked." God was irate about their garb because it reflected their hearts.

In Jerusalem, some women looked seductive. They shamelessly and immodestly sought to attract men's eyes. They were proud and flaunted themselves. God will judge women who dress alluringly to attract attention and create a lustful response.

God is warning us not only about putting bells on the feet, but about dressing to deliberately attract the gaze of the opposite sex, which is a sin. There may be no tinkling bells, but there are super-short skirts, low necklines, and tight clothes. These are clearly inconsistent with God's standard. God is very serious about how women dress. It is not wrong to look presentable and nice, but it is wrong to dress seductively. Adorning oneself for the sake of lust or to flaunt wealth is sin. Showy clothes, elaborate hairdos, and gaudy jewelry hardly express the humble heart that the Lord seeks. God is pleased by godly women, whose modest, quiet spirit is the true ornament of the heart.

The New Testament provides a comparable passage: "Do not let your adornment be merely outward—arranging the hair, wearing gold, or putting on fine apparel—rather let it be the hidden person of the heart, with the incorruptible beauty of a gentle and quiet spirit, which is very precious in the sight of God." (1Pet.3:3-4).

Here Peter is not talking against pigtails or ponytails. 1 Peter 3:3 could be interpreted as "gold-braided hair" rather than "braided hair" (NIV, ESV, ISV, ASV, WEB). He refers to spending too much time, money, and effort on clothes and hair. Women in Peter's day would often weave up to 110 braids in their hair braids. In each one they entwined silk cords with gold coins at irregular distances reaching down to the knees, so their hair glittered with every movement of the head. In fact, these sisters were stumbling blocks to the brothers. One ancient writer, Xenophon of Ephesus, described women with hair braided this way in a procession for the goddess Artemis and portrayed them as erotically attractive.

On their foreheads, some women also wore hollow horns of silver or gold, 18 to 20 inches long and adorned with a splash of precious stones. In the back, strong cords hung from the apparatus down to the knees, with tassels of red silk weighted with lead to keep the horns from falling forward. A further arrangement of cords and a strong band fixed tightly under the jaws, kept it firmly in place. In other words, they used elaborate effort to place their treasure on their head and on display. That is not at all what God wants, "but let it be the hidden man of the heart, the ornament of a meek and quiet spirit."

When Peter talks about braiding their hair, he also means women must choose clothes with discretion, modesty, and humility, and arrange their hair so it is not distracting. Coming to church otherwise will draw attention as well. The woman's true adornment lies in her beautiful heart and good character.

Another New Testament passage expresses the same meaning: "in like manner also, that the women adorn themselves in modest apparel, with propriety and moderation, not with braided hair or gold or pearls or costly clothing" (1Tim.2:9). "Modest" implies a certain sense of shame, though it doesn't mean you are ashamed of yourself. A brazen person is just flaunting oneself, with no sense of shame, but Paul means "modest" as the opposite of "brazen." Therefore, women have to garb themselves in modest apparel with godly fear, not in highly-coiffed hair gleaming with pearls and other costly ornaments. The character of godly women—not the outward fancy clothes—should draw attention. And there is no point in spending a lot of money on clothes you can get inexpensively.

Therefore, like Peter, Paul calls Christian women to an adornment that exalts God, especially in the time of worship. Our worship must come out of a humble and a contrite spirit. It is a time to give thanks to the Father, who has qualified us to be partakers of the inheritance of the saints in the light and delivered us from the power of darkness into the kingdom of His dear Son (Col.1:12-13). When you go to a wedding or formal party, you dress with respect, and so it is with church.

The first part of 1 Timothy 2:9 addresses women's appearance and the second part their attitude. A woman's adornment starts with the heart. In preparation for worship, women should experience godly fear and self-control. The word for "godly fear" here is *aidos*, meaning modesty mixed with humility.

This should be the attitude of every Christian woman. When women come together in the fellowship of redeemed saints to worship God, they are there for that purpose and everything they do as well as everything men do should draw our hearts toward God.

Men generally react to the visual. Therefore, the appearance of a woman will stimulate a man much more readily than the appearance of a man will stimulate a woman. Basically, that is just the way men are. When a woman walks around in an effort to attract the physical interest of men, Satan is using her to tempt them at their weakness. Some women do not understand that because they do not relate their own response to that of men.

In terms of fashion, says John MacArthur, "A Christian woman should not be the first to try it, nor the last to give it up, but somewhere in the middle. We should be presentable. There are some people who show spirituality with cheap and crummy clothes, and there are others who are on the leading edge of every new fashion. Christians should be somewhere in the middle. A godly woman is always balanced."

A Christian wife should attract attention to her godly character, not her clothing. She should show her love and devotion to her own husband by her dress and demeanor. There should not be any desire to entice men and exhibit her sensuality, but rather a sense of shame that befits true modesty and faithfulness to one's own husband. She should demonstrate a humble heart committed to worshiping God.

The same modesty and beauty of godly character should become her most attractive quality. Single women need to realize that the worship service is not the place to try to attract men. They should also understand that it is more important that men find them appealing for their godly character than their outward shell.

Indeed, women must make sure that they are coming for the purpose of worshiping God, and be exclusively committed to godly fear, with a sense of shame that they should ever tempt anyone.

How can married and single women know if they are dressed properly for the worship service? By examining their motives! A woman should ask herself: Why am I dressed this way? What is my object? Am I trying to draw attention to God or to myself? Will my clothing stand out or will it be considered appropriate?

Warren Henderson addresses women thus: "Who would you trying to impress? Certainly not the Lord! Show love to the brethren by not stumbling them in their thought-life. Choose to cover up instead of make up!" Clement of Alexandria summarizes this point candidly: "Love of display is not for a lady, but a prostitute."

Below is the dress code in the employee handbook of a Christian company in United States. The following are NOT appropriate attire:

- Shorts of any type (excluding tailored walking shorts and short suits, which must be no shorter than 4 inches above the top of the kneecap).
- Muscle shirts, halter tops, crop tops, tops which show any portion of the midriff, and tank tops.

- Sleeveless shirts (excluding tailored blouses and dresses).
- Dresses or skirts those are shorter than 4 inches above the top of the kneecap.
- Thong type sandals ("flip-flops").
- Foul, offensive, or controversial clothing and/or accessories.
- Sweat suits or jogging suits.
- Clothing with any visible holes or patches.
- Spandex pants, leggings, or low cut jeans without covering shirt or dress that covers the hips.
- Wide neck blouses, scoop neck tops, or deep cut v-neck tops can be very immodest. Careful discretion by the employee should be the rule.

Favorable personal appearance is an ongoing requirement of employment with the company. Employees who violate the Company's Appearance and Dress Codes may be asked to leave the workplace and change their appearance before returning to work. Failure to comply with these standards will result in disciplinary action.

And here is unacceptable attire in a U.S. retail pharmacy:
- Sweat pants
- Printed T-shirts with letters or pictures
- Midriff shirts
- Wrinkled pants, skirts or shirts
- Jeans
- Pants which are just below the knees or above the knees for ladies

If such attire is inappropriate in the business world, how can it be appropriate in church?

Chapter 17

The Place of Women in the Church

We are redeemed by the precious blood of Christ. Therefore, church is God's precious possession, the earthly expression of heaven, and reality on earth. "Knowing that you were not redeemed with corruptible things, like silver or gold...... but with the precious blood of Christ, as of a lamb without blemish and without spot." (1Pet.1:18-19). When Jesus looked at His church, He said, "You have given Me out of the world. They were Yours, You gave them to Me" (John 17:6). Hence, each individual redeemed, forgiven, and justified by the grace of God is a gift to the Son. As the church is a gift of God to the Christ, a woman is the gift of God to the man to carry out the ministry of God.

As Dr. Herbert Lockyer says, "The apostles set high standards for Christian women (1Tim.3:11; Titus 2:3-5, 1Pet.3:1-6) and exalt woman as a type of the Church, the Lamb's Bride (Eph.5:21-33). Later Tertullian wrote of the spiritual wealth and worthiness of Christian woman, and of how their modesty and simplicity was a rebuke to and reaction from the shameless extravagances and immoralities of heathen women. That they were among the most conspicuous examples of the transforming power of Christianity is manifest from the admiration and astonishment of the pagan Libanius who exclaimed, 'What women these Christians have!'"

With the feminist movement, we began facing many issues concerning the role of women in the church, such as: Can a woman teach men or exercise authority over men? Does the Bible allow women pastors or positions of ecclesiastical leadership? For almost the entire history of the church, the answer has been no.

Many contemporary churches of various denominations are promoting the idea that women are fully equal to men, without any distinctive roles in many areas like preaching or teaching. Therefore, women have the right to every office of ministry in the church.

We should never forget the fact that women are also included in the priesthood who worship God. The Bible specifically teaches that women have a place in the church. God uses both men and women to accomplish His purposes. In terms of spiritual life and blessing, men and women are equal. Although they are equal in Christ (Gal.3:28), women have a different role in the church. Serving God together is a key concept in the church. When men and women work jointly for the glory of God, they edify the body of Christ. As examples, we have many churches in the New Testament where there are servants or helpers and other functions for women to fulfill their God-given roles. It is a recognized fact, for instance, that there are more beautiful vocalists among women than men.

Among the Evangelical Christians, there are two main views in the gender debate: the complementarian and the egalitarian.

The Complementarian View

Complementarianism is the theological idea that God created men and women equally, with distinctive gender-defined roles in His image, and that they are fully equal in personhood, dignity, and value (Gen.1:26-28). It is rooted in more literal interpretations of the Creation account and the roles of men and women described in Scripture. It is also known as the traditionalist or hierarchical view.

They chose the name "complementarian" to emphasize both the equality of the sexes and the complementary differences between men and women. Complementarians teach that all born-again Christians—male or female—are equal members of the body of Christ, and therefore they should use their spiritual gifts to their greatest potential and grow into full spiritual maturity.

In addition, complementarians believe that God created men and women differently, and they have to carry out distinct gender roles. God made man to be the responsible head of the home and to provide godly leadership in the home and in the church. God made woman to be the helper for man and she is to submit to the man's leadership in church and at home.

Complementarians believe that the correct teaching of the Bible on gender holds both truths—equal-yet-different (equality with role differences)—and this view best stands for God's infallible truth and intelligent design for the good of His people and His glory. These truths are to be preserved in balance as part of God's original purpose prior to the fall.

The complementarian view is promoted by the Council for Biblical Manhood and Womanhood (CBMW). Some well-known complementarian theologians and authors are: Gleason Archer, Mark Dever Jr., Mark Driscoll, Elizabeth Elliot, John M. Frame, Wayne Grudem, H. Wayne House, R. Kent Hughes, James Hurley, Mary Kassian, George W. Knight, Richard Land, C.S. Lewis, John F. MacArthur, C. J. Mahaney, R. Albert Mohler, J. I. Packer, Dorothy Patterson, John Piper, Adrian Rogers, Charles C. Ryrie, R. C. Sproul, Terry Virgo, and John Walvoord.

The Egalitarian View

The English word "egalitarian" is derived from the French *égal* or "equal." Egalitarians teach that God created man and woman fully equal and that true equality demands equal offices in the church and equal marital roles in the home. It is also called Biblical feminism, or Biblical equality. Egalitarians believe in deciding leadership and teaching in the church by spiritual gifts and not by gender. Therefore, all have an equal responsibility to use their gifts for God's glory and there should be no limits on women's roles.

Egalitarians also believe that the statements in the Bible on headship and submission have been misinterpreted, and they give more importance to the equality of men and women (Gen.1:26-28; Gal.3:28). Moreover, they think that equal-yet-different, as taught by complementarians, is a contradiction and that male domination of women is the result of the fall (Gen.3).

Egalitarians have taken the statement in Galatians 3:28 ("there is neither male nor female; for you are all one in Christ Jesus.") out of context to deduce that it relates to female participation in church activities. But this verse refers to sonship in God's family (Eph.1:3), not service in the assembly. There are "male and female" in the church—otherwise, the exhortations to husbands and wives in the Bible (Eph.5:22-33, 1Pet.3:1, Col.3:18, Titus 2:5; Gen.3:16) would be meaningless. It is God who established marriage and gave dominion to husband over wife (Gen.2:23-24).

The egalitarian view is promoted by Christians for Biblical Equality (CBE). The CBE began with women who had withdrawn from the Evangelical Women's Caucus (because of a disagreement over the issue of endorsing lesbianism). Some prominent egalitarians are: D. Stuart Briscoe, F.F. Bruce, Gilbert Bilezikian, Anthony Campolo, Millard J. Erickson, Gordon Fee, Stanley Grenz, Rebecca Groothius, Vernon Grounds, William J. Hybels, Kenneth S. Kantzer, Craig S. Keener, Catherine Clark Kroeger, Richard J. Mouw, Grant R. Osborne, Carroll Osburn, Philip Barton Payne, Cornelius Plantiga Jr., Ruth Tucker, William Webb, and Ben Witherington III.

Women's Silence in the Assembly

When Christ liberated women, the women from pagan cultures began to misuse their freedom in the assembly. Therefore, in 1 Corinthians 14, Apostle Paul deals with the topic of head covering first and then woman's silence in the church: "Let your women keep silent in the churches, for they are not permitted to speak; but they are to be submissive, as the law also says" (1Cor.14:34-35).

The word used there for "silent" in Greek is *sigatosan*, which means "let them be silent."

In 1 Timothy 2:11-14, Paul reminds the sisters of the injunction of Holy Spirit to learn quietly. "Let the woman learn in silence with all subjection. But I suffer not a woman to teach, nor to usurp authority over the man, but to be in silence. For Adam was first formed, then Eve. And Adam was not deceived, but the woman being deceived was in the transgression."

The term for "silence" in the original tongue is *en hisuchia*. The reasons given by Paul are twofold (1Tim.2:13-14), based on creation and the fall:

1) Adam was formed first, then Eve—therefore, man has the authority.

2) Adam was not deceived, although he transgressed willfully, but Eve was deceived.

Isn't Paul saying that women generally can more easily be fooled than men, and therefore they ought not to teach? And the likelihood of imparting false instruction rises when women begin to teach over the men? Our assemblies are blessed with many gifted women who can illuminate the scriptures in sisters' meetings, Sunday school, women's retreats and in circumstances where no men teachers are available, such as missionary situations. But in the presence of men, women should surrender their role to them. Therefore, in assembly gatherings, women are not to teach or exercise authority in the presence of men.

God did not design women to teach men in the church, but they are to learn. They are not to take authority in the church and rule over men because they are a weaker vessel in both roles, as leaders and teachers in the spiritual realm.

God made Adam first, and then He made Eve to be a helper for Adam. Furthermore, Adam was not deceived but the woman was, and transgressed. The woman is the submissive one by creation and, being a weaker vessel, was tricked when she attempted to deal independently with the enemy. This confirms her submissive role and reinforces the need for a male leader. The German theologian Werner Neuer remarked, "The fall is therefore, not only the rebellion of mankind against God, but the setting aside of the divinely appointed order of male and female." Isaiah asserts that women's ruling over men is a sign of God's judgment: "As for My people, children are their oppressors, and women rule over them. O My people! Those who lead you cause you to err, and destroy the way of your paths." (Isa.3:12).

When Paul says emphatically, "And if they want to learn something, let them ask their own husbands at home; for it is shameful for women to speak in church." (1Cor.14:35), that doesn't mean a woman cannot give a testimony or read a portion from the scripture. But women are not to take on a role of ruling or being teachers in the church. If they need to know anything, let them learn by asking their husbands. Men have great responsibility because a woman's greatest spiritual resource is a man. Therefore, men should learn the Word of God—for themselves and for their wives. Most of the husbands' problems arise when women come to ask questions of them and they don't know the answer! In that case, they can ask the teachers in the church. That's why God has provided gifted pastors and teachers in the church: to teach and equip the congregation (Eph.4:11).

Aquila and Priscilla were very devoted to teaching others. They were willing to sacrifice much in giving up their home for a church as well as inviting the eloquent Apollos to their home and explaining the way of God to him more clearly (Acts 18:26-28).

The fact that women are to be silent doesn't mean that they cannot talk about God or biblical truths to others. God had used Miriam (Exod.15:20-21), Deborah the prophetess (Judges 4:4), and Huldah (2 Kings 22:14-22) to speak for God, and Anna spoke about Lord's Christ to all who were looking forward to the redemption of Jerusalem (Luke 2:36-38).

Women's silence in 1 Corinthians 14 has been misinterpreted in two ways.

1. Some critics who believe in letting women preach in the church interpret "silence" as a reference to a meek and quiet spirit and they claim that women preachers or teachers must have such a spirit.

2. Others go to the opposite extreme and insist that no woman should ever talk in church under any circumstances. But if so, how can they sing to the Lord, say amen, read psalms, or praise God?

Paul makes very clear in 1 Timothy 2:12 what he means by "silence." Women are to be silent in the sense of not teaching or exercising over men in the church. They are to learn in silence (1Cor.14:34). 1 Corinthians 14:34 embodies the thought of 1 Timothy 2:11. There Paul writes, "Let your women keep silent in the churches, for they are not permitted to speak; but they are to be submissive, as the law also says."

Throughout the Bible, we nowhere find God appointing a woman to be a national leader, prophet, priest, or king in Israel. Although Deborah was judge in Israel, she was not like other judges, who delivered Israel. When the time came to deliver Israel, she understood her calling and encouraged Barak to lead the battle. God used Barak to deliver them. In the list of faith warriors, we find Barak's name, and not Deborah's (Heb.11:32).

As Wayne Grudem and John Piper explain, "(1) Deborah is a special case because she seems to be the only judge in Judges who has no military function. The other judges also lead Israel into victory in battle, but Deborah receives a word from the Lord that Barak is to do this (Judges 4:6-7). Deborah is not asserting leadership for herself; she gives priority to a man. (2) There is an implied rebuke of Barak because he is not willing to go to battle without Deborah (Judges 4:8). Because of his reluctance, the glory that day will go to a woman (Judges 4:9), but note that the woman is not Deborah but Jael (Judges 4:17ff.). In other words, Deborah did speak the word of God, but her attitude and demeanor were such that she was not asserting her leadership. Instead, she handed over the leadership, contrary to the pattern of all the other judges, to a man."

The Bible came from some 40 different authors from diverse vocations in life. And of the 66 books of the Bible, none was written by a woman. God chose all men. Therefore it is evident that God doesn't want a woman to take authority over man in the sense of teaching.

As C.H. Mackintosh notes, "We would just express our ever deepening conviction that home is, pre-eminently, the woman's sphere. There she can shine whether as a wife, a mother or a mistress (home manager), to the glory of Him who has called her to fill those holy relationships. There the loveliest traits of female character are developed—traits which are completely defaced when she abandons her home work and enter the domain of the public preacher. We believe it is plainly opposed to Scripture for a woman to speak in the Church, or to teach, or in any way, usurp authority over the man. But if there be a meeting of a private, social character, there is, in our judgment, an opening for the free communication of the thought provided always that the woman keep the place assigned her by the voice of nature and the Word of God."

Warren Henderson illustrates the headship principle in the early church from Acts 21: "Paul was refreshing himself in the home of Philip for a few days before traveling to Jerusalem. Acts 21:9 records the fact that Philip had four virgin daughters who prophesied. Although it is true that these women had the gift of prophecy, there is no evidence they ever used this gift in the church meetings. Prophecy is not limited to church meetings any more than prayer is. It should also be pointed out that God used an older male prophet, Agabus, who had to travel about 40 miles to exhort Paul, instead of using Philip's daughters who were not only in the same city, but within the same house that Paul was staying. It would have been much simpler to have one of Philip's daughters rebuke Paul; instead God summoned Agabus. This demonstrates the principle of diving headship. It would have broken God's order to have a woman instruct the Apostle."

Craig Keener has a different view: "Women were less likely to be literate than men. Given women's lack of training in the Scriptures, the heresy spreading in the Ephesian churches through ignorant teachers (1Tim.1:4-7), and the false teachers' exploitation of these women's lack of knowledge to spread their errors (1Tim.5:13; 2Tim.3:6), Paul's prohibition makes good sense. His short-range solution is that these women should not teach; his long-range solution is 'let them learn' (1Tim.2:11). The situation might be different after the women had been instructed

(1Tim.2:11; cf. Rom.16:1-4, 7; Phil.4:2-3)."

When Paul writes in 1Timothy 2:11, "Let a woman learn in silence," he means that women are not to teach during the official meeting of the church. God does not permit women to teach in the presence of men, or usurp authority over man (1Cor.14:34, 1Tim.2:12), since man is the head of the women. The responsibility of being the preacher, the teacher, or the one who leads in prayer is a role ordained for men.

God has entrusted many gifted women to teach the Word of God, but God does not permit them to teach in the presence of men. Although there's no difference in sex in Christ, as long as we are in the flesh, there is a distinction between man and woman; therefore, woman is subject to man in the church.

In the new creation, both men and women are equally part of the bride of the church and will reign with Christ as bride. The redemption of our body will be complete only when we receive our glorified body at the second coming of our Lord.

William Kelly observes, "These are earthly roles, not roles of the new creation where there are no distinctions between men and women (Gal.3:28). Both equally are going to heaven, both equally have the Holy Spirit, and one or more spiritual gifts. Both equally belong to the assembly. Both equally are part of the bride of Christ. Both equally will reign with Him as His wife."

Let's summarize the meaning of women's silence, the reason for it and the source of subjection.

◆ *The meaning of women's silence*

The context of 1 Corinthians 14:34 indicates that Paul did not intend his injunction on silence to prevent women from speaking at all, but to keep them from speaking in tongues and prophesying in the church.

◆ *The reason for women's silence*

The reason women are not to teach or preach in the church has nothing to do with their intellectual capabilities or anatomical and psychological structures, but rather God's law forbids it (1Cor.14:34; cf. Gen.3:16).

◆ *The source of subjection*

The head of every man is Christ and God the Father is the head of Christ. Christ took upon Himself the form of a servant during His Incarnation (Phil.2:5-8). Therefore subjection is not inferiority.

Women do have the gift of teaching or leadership, but it is not God's design for them to exercise their spiritual gift of teaching over men. They are to use those talents among women and children. This harmonizes with Paul's instructions to older women in Titus 2:3. Therefore, it is textually wrong to conclude that there is no restriction on women in ministry from Paul's teaching. Under the direction of the leadership and in the right setting, there is nothing wrong with a woman sharing (not teaching) what the Holy Spirit has taught her. Women can proclaim the Word of God at any place (sisters' meetings, children's meetings, Sunday school) except when the church comes together.

The Ministry of Women

Throughout the Bible, the ministry of women was complementary and supportive of the male leadership in the church. It was notable and significant, but it never replaced the male ministry. Men sometimes have suppressed the valuable contributions of women for various reasons. There are numerous ministries in which a woman can participate to advance the kingdom of God; nevertheless they should always be complementary and supportive of the male leadership in the home and in the church. Although there are few limitations on women in ministry, let me describe some of the more important ministries of women in the church and in the community.

1. Prayer

Prayer is indispensable in the assembly for its blessing, edification, and very existence. In the church, many more Christian women than men are prayer warriors. In addition, they are often the spiritual heart of the home – encouraging and praying.

They may be unknown to men, but they are well known to God. Women spend more time fasting and praying for missionaries, evangelists, sick ones, and children, and seeking the edification and growth of the church.

2. Financial Support

Sisters are the ones who give generously to the Lord's work. We do not know how much they support the poor, needy, sick, and the evangelists. The Father, who sees secretly, will reward them at the judgment seat (Matt.6:3-4). For example, when a poor widow came and placed two mites in the treasury, Jesus said that she donated more than the rest combined: "Assuredly, I say to you that this poor widow has put in more than all those who have given to the treasury; for they all put in out of their abundance, but she out of her poverty put in all that she had, her whole livelihood" (Mark 12:43-44).

3. Attendance in Meetings

We can assume that attendance at most meetings would be less than 50 percent if the sisters were not present. They are the ones who encourage their own husbands and others to attend. They are indispensable!

4. Making an Impact on Their Husbands and Children

Countless mothers and wives have had a lasting effect on their husbands and children, and we still do not fully know the influence of these women. A mother is someone who can take the place of all others, but whose place no one else can take.

In a "Tribute to Emma Moody," Warren Henderson highlighted one woman's impact: "She sought her husband's welfare in all matters and co-labored with him continuously. Besides attending to the wounded and the distressed soldiers, she assisted the Sunday School mission and was busy visiting the poor, keeping the home in good order, and attending to guests, including D.L. Moody's chronically ill brother, Samuel.

"While on his death bed, Mr. Moody turned his eyes to gaze upon his beloved Emma and softly uttered, 'Mamma, you have been a good wife to me.' The fact that all their children went on to impact the next generation for the Lord is an outstanding testimony of Emma Moody's maternal ministry."

5. Sunday School, Good News Club, VBS, and Children's Ministry

Women can also have a powerful ministry with children in the church. There are so many people who accept the Lord as their Savior through Sunday Schools, VBS, Good News Clubs, and other spiritual activities, but only eternity will reveal the results of those who have come to the Lord through the ministry of sisters. The majority of sisters who teach in the Sunday Schools and involve themselves in the Good News Clubs are committed. Although men are needed to work with children, God has mainly designed women for this important role. We need women who love children and can help mold them.

6. Writing

Women can exercise their creative gifts through writing, translating, editing, and proofreading. I am extremely impressed by a dedicated sister in the Lord, Mrs. Annie Wilson, whose knowledge, wisdom, and creative insights have greatly enhanced this book and been an indispensable support to me in publishing it. In our day, women have written a number of Christian books, as well as many of the hymns that inspire our hearts and refresh our minds.

7. Witnessing

We read that "Great were the company of those [women] who proclaimed it" (Psalms 68:11). Many women have access to places where men cannot reach. When Paul lists his co-laborers, eight out of 26 were women (Rom.15). Women can influence many in hospitals and other workplaces.

It is highly noteworthy that the chief witnesses to the empty tomb of Jesus are women who were followers of Jesus. With regard to the uniqueness of the circumstance, and as all three synoptic gospel writers say with the utmost assurance, we can conclude that all four women went to the tomb: Mary Magdalene, Salome, Joanna and the wife of Cleophas.

Women were the first witnesses to the empty tomb of Jesus because they had gone to the tomb to anoint Jesus with the prepared spices in the pre-dawn morning, an act that shows their love, fidelity, and commitment to their master. As William MacDonald states, "The faithfulness and devotion of women at the crucifixion and resurrection of our Lord should be noticed. The disciples had forsaken the Lord and fled." It was to Mary Magdalene that Jesus appeared first after his resurrection, and became what one observer has called 'the apostle to the apostles.'"

The conservative Thomas Schreiner writes, "Even though the testimony of women was not received by courts... Jesus appeared to women first, showing again their significance and value as human beings."

Borland, also a conservative, adds, "Why were the women chosen as witnesses of the resurrection? Was God bestowing a special honor on these women? Was God trying to indicate larger roles for women in His new community of believers? I believe both were intended. All four Gospel writers bestow a great honor on the women who lovingly and with servant hearts came early to the tomb to anoint Jesus' body, thus paying their last respects.... These women led the way in proclaiming the gospel.... The duty and high privilege of witnessing for Christ is still open to every believer, without distinction as to gender."

8. Good Works

Women are God's workmanship created in Christ Jesus to do good works (Eph.2:10). Without them, the world would have an incomplete picture of God. Dorcas (Tabitha) was known for her lifetime of good works. She made coats and garments for widows (Acts 9:36, 39), and Dr. Herbert Lockyer says, "Here was a woman who with her needle embroidered her name ineffaceably into the beneficence of the world." She could have possibly learnt it in a godly home where she was taught how to use her talents for the comfort and relief of those in need. Luke gives us some indications of her witness and work in his historical account. No matter what your position is on this earth, whether as man or woman, educated or uneducated, you can be used mightily for the Lord.

9. The Older Women's Mandate: To Teach the Younger Ones

The church has great need of theologically sound women to instruct younger females. God has a wonderful design for women, briefly stated in Titus 2:4-5: "That they admonish the young women to love their husbands, to love their children, to be discreet, chaste, homemakers, good, obedient to their own husbands, that the word of God may not be blasphemed." Older women are thus given a clear mandate that will make them a blessing to the world, bring fulfillment to their own lives, and realize God's purpose to the glory of God. If older women are obedient, they should take up the responsibility to teach younger women.

Apostle Paul was training his young disciple Titus, a young man. He was told to teach the older women to teach the younger ones. Timothy is addressing the young women in the church because they have had a tendency to ignore their responsibilities at home. The reason is that the sin of man caused everything to come under the curse of God, which brought consequences (Gen.3:13-24). One is that "her desire would be towards her husband," and another is "he shall rule over her" (Gen.3:16). The word "desire" in the original tongue means "to dominate" or to "rule." Because of the fall, the woman's natural desire is to dominate her husband and the husband's desire is to rule his wife. As a result, family battles can arise and ultimately only the power of the Holy Spirit resolves them. Therefore, older women need to remind young ones that there is something in the fallen flesh that wants to dominate, which can only be overcome by the Holy Spirit. (Equality and role differences are the truths to be maintained in balance, as part of God's original intent prior to the fall into sin.)

Matthew Henry observes, "It is to be sadly lamented by every one of us that we brought into the world with us a corrupt nature, wretchedly degenerated from its primitive purity and rectitude; we have from our birth the snares of sin in our bodies, the seeds of sin in our souls, and a stain of sin upon both. This is what we call original sin, because it is ancient as our original, and because it is the original of all our actual transgressions."

Furthermore, philosopher Peter Kreeft provides a poignant picture of our body stained by the fall: "The Fall turned things upside down between soul and body. Before the fall, the body was a transparent window, a totally malleable instrument, a perfectly obedient servant of the soul."

Only the resurrection restores this relationship. Therefore older women are given the responsibility of teaching young females the self-discipline that enables them to do their duty, "to love their husbands, love their children, and other virtues." Older women need to engage themselves in the training process to bring about a generation of disciplined, prudent women who are committed to doing God's will. What we lack today are gifted women to counsel the young generation.

The older women should have the quality mentioned in 1Timothy 3:11: "must be reverent, not slanderers, temperate, faithful in all things." Older women should strive to be like the woman portrayed in Proverbs 31. If she is full of good works like Dorcas, she will not have much time to spend in gossip.

Older women who no longer have the responsibility of their own children now have the task of training the next generation of women. Older women have made bad choices and they can teach the young ones how to avoid them through the valuable lessons they have learned in life. "If you are an empty nester and you have been faithful as a wife and mother, you have been commissioned by God to a teaching ministry," says Warren Henderson. "Experience is a great teacher, and these older sisters had a wealth of practical knowledge in domestic affairs to pass down to the younger women. Such instruction would lessen the possibility of new wife and mother needlessly repeating the past mistakes of others."

In the first-century church, certain widows acted as official servants of the church and carried out a number of tasks. They regularly visited the younger women of the church to teach them, aid them in daily routines, guide them to wisdom, and help them be good mothers and homemakers. They had an ongoing responsibility to be available to those women in the church who needed their assistance.

They also provided teaching and counseling when a specific need arose. They visited the sick, the afflicted, and the imprisoned, and they provided hospitality to traveling preachers, evangelists, missionaries, and Christians who might come to town because of persecution elsewhere.

Second, "Teach young women to love their children." Although it is natural for a mother to love her children, it is of great importance that a Christian mother has a certain vision for them. "She has them in her care for only a few years," Anne Barnett writes, "and in those years she must help them to prepare for the life which lies before them. She will realize that her child is a gift from God, and then she will be happy to bring him up to serve God, as Hannah did, 1 Samuel 1:28." Without the love of earthly parents, how can a child learn the love of heavenly Father?

A woman's highest calling is to raise godly children. "Nevertheless she will be saved in childbearing if they continue in faith, love, and holiness, with self-control" (1Timothy 2:15). Such children will reverse the consequence of sin by which women are dishonored because one woman led the mankind into sin. They will also be preserved from that stigma when they rear a godly generation.

Third, "Teach the young women to be pure." "Pure" means chaste, innocent, and clean. It refers sexual purity—faithfulness to husband. Older women need to teach the young women to be devoted to one man. "Let the wife make her husband glad to come home," said Martin Luther, "and let him make her sorry to see him leave."

Fourth, Paul says women should be "keepers at home," meaning guardians at home. Nowadays many women do not want to be keepers at home. Yet the sphere of a woman's ministry *is* her home. It is where a woman provides the expression of love for her husband and her children. It is where she leads, guides, and raises the godly generation. The home is where she can keep herself untarnished by the world and secure from other men. It is also where she lodges strangers, shows hospitality, and devotes herself to every good work.

John Wesley listed seven factors he desired in a wife, and among them are her excellence as a "housekeeper, nurse, companion, friend, and a fellow laborer in the gospel of Christ."

Fifth, "She should be kind" (v.5). In other words, a woman should be gentle, tender-hearted, merciful, and compassionate. Only the compassionate can truly encourage the broken-hearted and make a huge uplifting impact on the lives of others.

And sixth, younger women need to be "obedient to their own husbands" or "subject to their own husbands" (Eph.5:22). That is, not somebody else's, but their own. They submit to the order God designed. "A woman doesn't know how to bow her knee to God," says John MacArthur, "until she learns how to bow her knee to her husband."

Charles Haddon Spurgeon wrote this tribute to his wife: "She delights in her husband, in his person, his character, his affection. To her he is not only the chief and foremost of mankind, but in her eyes he is all and all. Her heart's love belongs to him and to him only. He is her little world, her paradise, her choice treasure. She is glad to sink her individuality in him. She seeks no renown for herself. His honor is reflected upon her and she rejoices in it. She will defend his name with her dying breath. Safe enough is he where she can speak for him. His smiling gratitude is all the reward she seeks."

Listen to Warren Wiersbe on God's plan for family order: "God does all things decently and in order (1Cor.14:40). If He did not have a chain of command in society, we would have chaos. The fact that the woman is to submit to her husband does not suggest that the man is better then the woman. It only means that the man has the responsibility of headship and leadership in the home. Headship is not dictatorship or lordship. It is loving leadership. In fact, both the husband and the wife must be submitted to the Lord and to each other (Eph.5:21). It is a mutual respect under the lordship of Jesus Christ.

"True spiritual submission is the secret of growth and fulfillment. When a Christian woman is submitted to the Lord and to her own husband, she experiences a release and fulfillment that she can have in no other way. This mutual love and submission creates an atmosphere of growth in the home that enables both the husband and the wife to become all that God wants them to be. The fact that the Christian wife is in the Lord is not an excuse for selfish independence. Just the opposite is true, for her salvation makes it important that she obey the Word and submit to her husband."

Precious women who respected the authority of their husbands:

1. Sarah, who called Abraham Lord, respected his authority, and obeyed him (1Pet.3:6).
2. Rebecca, when she took a veil on seeing Isaac and covered herself to show her respect for his authority (Gen.21:2).
3. Rachel and Leah, who affirmed Jacob's leadership by listening to him (Gen.31:14-16).

Women who did not respect their husbands:

1. Eve, who without counseling Adam dealt with the enemy, was tempted and deceived, and led Adam into sin (Gen.3:6).
2. Rebecca, when she took over Isaac's God-given authority (Gen. 27:5-13).
3. Job's wife, who told him to curse God and die (Job 2:9).

10. Social Activities

For occasions like fellowship meetings, social gatherings, and picnics, the assembly depends upon sisters to prepare food. Moreover, in most cases they are the ones who take the initiative in entertaining guests, evangelists, and strangers.

11. Visiting the Sick, Orphans, and Widows

God can use you to bless a stranger with a friendly smile and a helping hand. He inspires you to speak words of blessing as they are lonely or depressed. It will flow through the heart and fresh up the mind with divine light and hope. It's a legacy of joy you can pass on to others. James says, "Pure and undefiled religion before God and the Father is this: to visit orphans and widows in their trouble" (1:27). As Christians we have to make impacts, not impressions. Matthew says, "I was sick and you visited Me" (25:36). Visiting the sick and elderly, helping the disabled, counseling the troubled and confused—these activities are open to all, including elders, teachers, deacons, evangelists, and sisters. Ministering to them with a compassionate heart will influence them more deeply than a sermon.

12. Community Help

Christian women always have provided valuable services to the community. God has shaped them with special gifts of service needed for the common good. Many Christian Professional women who have fewer responsibilities at home and with the family go forth and enrich the community in roles such as camp counselor. They also can help the needy after natural disasters or in the face of distressing medical problems like cancer or HIV. If God has given them creative insights into arts and crafts, they may offer art activities to patients at the local children's hospital. As we are salt of the earth and light of the world, volunteering lets us focus on others and see that our service to the community can be meaningful. Jesus Christ said, "Let your light so shine before men, that they may see your good works and give glory to your Father who is in heaven" (Matt.5:16).

13. Servants of the Church (Deaconesses)

Everybody in the church serves in one way or another. In some churches, women with very special gifts serve in an office, although it is disputed that they functioned in official positions. The term "deaconess" is commonly used, though there is no Greek term for it. Those who serve under the direction of the elders in any function of ministry must have the qualifications of the scripture, because that is the group of people called for spiritual service. "Any sister who serves in connection with a local assembly can be a 'deaconess,'" says William MacDonald.

In the early second century, the Roman governor Pliny tells of inflicting agony on a pair of Christian women: "This made me decide it was all the more necessary to extract the truth by torture from two slave-women, whom they called deaconesses. I found nothing but a degenerate sort of cult carried to extravagant lengths" (Pliny, *Letters to Trajan* 10.96-97).

In the Bible, the ministry of a woman called Phoebe appears in Romans 16:1: "I commend to you our sister Phoebe, a deaconess (*diakonon, diakonos*) of the church at Cen'chre-ae" (RSV). H.A. Ironside says, "In Romans 16, we find the feminine word for deacon. The apostle sent his epistle by the hand of a lady who was traveling to Rome and he calls her 'Phoebe, our sister, who is a servant of the church at Cenchrea.' She served the church. So a woman who serves the church is called in Scripture, a 'Deaconess'" (1 and 2 Timothy, Titus, and Philemon).

"Phoebe was recognized by the church for her service," notes John MacArthur. "It's possible she served in an official capacity as a deaconess at the church in Cenchrea."

Dr. Herbert Lockyer concludes, "We can safely assume that Phoebe was one of the first, if not the first, of the noble band of deaconesses in the Christian Church. If hers was not an official ministry, it was certainly a most gracious and effective one, and she was indeed one of the forerunners of the vast army of women who have rendered such loyal service to Christ and His Church."

From linguistic and chronological argument, Charles Ryrie argues that Phoebe held no official position in the church. Ryrie's chronological argument is that by the time of the writing of the epistle to the Romans there is no indication that the official diaconate had been established at Corinth, of which Cenchrea was the eastern port. (Ryrie, *Role of Women*, 88).

Alexander Strauch suggests that the term is figurative: "In all probability, Paul is commending her for extraordinary service by means of the beautiful description, 'servant of the church.' Paul and Luke customarily describe others by their work or faithfulness, not by official titles. If Paul is calling Phoebe a 'deacon of the church,' it would be a unique exception to his usual practice" (*New Testament Deacon*, 177 n. 3).

Wayne Grudem and John Piper elaborate: "Paul says that she was a deaconess, of the church in Cenchreae (RSV). Actually, the word deaconess here is the same as the one used in 1 Timothy 3:8 and Philippians 1:1, where Paul writes of deacons. Thus, Paul is not calling Phoebe a 'deaconess,' but a 'deacon,' some have claimed. In addition, Phoebe is called a leader (*prostatis*) in Romans 16:2. The most commonly used translations (KJV, NASB, NIV) use the word 'help' or 'helper' here, but it has been claimed that this term is a technical one used for a legal protector or leader. If such an interpretation is accurate, Paul here commends Phoebe as a deacon and as a leader of many. All of this evidence is in accord with Paul's designation of women as fellow-workers in the gospel."

Some theologians limit the office of deacon to men and believe that the best interpretation of the women mentioned in 1 Timothy 3:11 is that they are the wives of the deacons. Among those who favor this view are Charles Ryrie, Alexander Strauch, Dan Doriani, Daniel B. Wallace, George W. Knight and Mal Couch. Those who favor female deacons include Ann Bowman, John Benton, Wayne House, James Hurley, John MacArthur, Werner Neuer, and Charles Swindoll.

Among the godly women who served our Lord and the Apostles are:

◆ Martha, who received the Lord into her house and showed hospitality (Luke 10:38; John 12:2).

◆ Peter's mother-in-law, who ministered to our Lord and His disciples (Mark 1:31).

◆ The mother of Rufus, who was a helper and encouragement to Paul (Rom.16:13).

◆ Euodia and Syntyche, who labored with Paul in gospel work.

◆ Women who labored with Paul in the gospel (Phil.4:3).

◆ Joanna, Susanna, and many others who ministered our Lord with their substance (Luke 8:3). (Joanna was the wife of Herod's personal steward.)

Should we include Claudia, the wife of Roman procurator Pontius Pilate, in the circle of His followers? Not in the sense of actual discipleship, but in some mysterious way she had come under the influence of His moral and spiritual radiance. It was Claudia who helped induce Pilate to stand for justice and weigh the truth until the very last moment (Matt.27:19). In fact, God used Claudia to sway Pilate to declare the truth that Jesus was a righteous man as he delivered Him in the hands of Jews to be crucified.

14. House Churches

Mary, the mother of John Mark opened her house for the gathering of saints in Jerusalem (Acts 12:12). The first convert in Europe, in Philippi, was a woman named Lydia, and she opened her home for the Lord (Acts 16:15). Priscilla and Aquila were very devoted. They entertained Paul in their house and they worked together—by trade they were tent makers. They sacrificially gave up their house for the kingdom of God and risked their lives for the Lord (Acts 18:4-26; 1Cor.16:19; Rom.16:5). Paul tells of the house churches of Apphia in Philemon 2 and Nympha of Laodicea in Colossians 4:15.

Although there were house churches in woman's homes, it is unclear who the leaders of the church were. According to Wayne Grudem and John Piper, "The church met in Mary's house in Acts 12:12, but there is no reason to think Mary was the leader of the church in that situation."

Conclusion

A woman can become involved in numerous ministries to advance the kingdom of God, such as by providing instruction for younger ones, financial support, prayer, Sunday school help, mentoring to other women (Titus 2:4-5), ministry to children, missionary work, gospel outreach, visits to sick ones, aid to the poor, and food and clothes to the needy. In the scripture, we nowhere find God anointing a woman to be a prophet, priest, or king. He called only men to be apostles of the early church. In the assembly, only men are qualified to be leaders, elders, and deacons (Titus 1:6; 1Tim.3:1-2, 3:11-12; Acts 6:3), and women are helpers, encouragers, and even teachers to other women and children (Titus 2:4-5; 2Tim.1:5; 3:14-15).

"Scripture never discounts the female intellect, downplays the talents and abilities of women, or discourages the right use of women's spiritual gifts," says John MacArthur. "But whenever the Bible expressly talks about the marks of an excellent woman, the stress is always on feminine *virtue*. The most significant women in Scripture were influential not because of their careers, but because of their *character*. The message these women collectively give is not about 'gender equality'; it's about true feminine excellence. And that is always exemplified in moral and spiritual qualities rather than by social standing, wealth, or physical appearance." (*Twelve Extraordinary Women*)

Appendix

Church History

(Excerpts from Apostolic Fathers, Reformers and Theologians)

Apostolic fathers are contemporaries of the apostles who became the church leaders and writers of the first and early second centuries. Some probably had personal contacts with the apostles, fellowshipped with them, and learned from them, or were close to others who had known the apostles. Therefore there is a strong possibility that their teachings trace back to the apostles themselves.

These church leaders and theologians may differ about the relevance of the head covering, but all of them strongly agree that the head covering mentioned in 1 Corinthians 11:4, 5, 6, 7, 10, 13 was not just hair, but a garment for women to wear in spiritual gatherings. The following are the teachings of apostolic fathers, reformers, and theologians on head covering.

A. Apostolic Fathers
1. Irenaeus (120-202 A.D)

Around 185, the early church father Irenaeus translated 1 Corinthians 11:10 thus: "A woman ought to have a veil [*kalumma*] upon her head, because of the angels." This is significant since Irenaeus apparently understood the "power" on a woman's head in 1Corinthians 11:10 to be a fabric of some kind and not a woman's hair. (*Against Heresies*, Book 1, 8:2, cited in *The Ante-Nicene Fathers*, A. Cleveland Cox, ed., U.S.A: The Christian Literature Publishing Co., 1885, I:327)

2. Tertullian (150-225 A.D)

Referring to 1Corinthians 11:4-5 around 200 CE, the African church father Tertullian states, "Behold two diverse names, Man and Woman 'every one' in each case: two laws, mutually distinctive; on the one hand (a law) of veiling, on the other (a law) of baring."

Tertullian's witness is highly significant. It unmistakably shows that in North Africa, Greece, and elsewhere at this time, Christian women were expected to have long hair that they would veil or cover when praying. It thus clearly demonstrates that the situation was not just a local matter in Corinth or that it was mere custom. It was, in fact, considered as "the law of veiling the head." (On The Veiling Of Virgins, cited in *The Ante-Nicene Fathers*, A. Cleveland Cox, ed., U.S. A.: The Christian Literature Publishing Co., 1885, IV:32)

3. Clement of Alexandria (153-217 A.D.)

Clement also has the same opinion that 1Corinthians 11:5 refer to a veil of fabric and not to hair: "And she will never fall, who puts before her eyes modesty, and her shawl; nor will she invite another to fall into sin by uncovering her face. For this is the wish of the Word, since it is becoming for her to pray veiled." (1Corinthians 11:5, GLP). (The Instructor, cited in *The Ante-Nicene Fathers*, A. Cleveland Cox, ed., U.S.A: The Christian Literature Publishing Co.,1885, II:290)

4. Hippolytus (170-236 A.D)

Hippolytus was a church leader of Rome. The following statement is taken from a record of various customs and practices he compiled:

"And let all the women have their heads covered with an opaque cloth, not with a veil of thin linen, for this is not a true covering (*Hippolytus Apostolic Tradition*)

5. John Chrysostom (340-407 A. D.)

Chrysostom was the notable preacher of Antioch. He describes the problem Paul addresses in 1 Corinthians 11:2-16 thus: "Their women used to pray and prophesy unveiled and with their head bare."

On the issue of whether a woman needs fabric rather than just hair (cf. 1Cor.11:15), he observes, "'And if it be given her for a covering,' say you, 'wherefore need she add another covering?' That not nature only, but also her own will may have part in her acknowledgment of subjection. For that thou oughtest to be covered nature herself by anticipation enacted a law. Add now, I pray, thine own part also, that thou mayest not seem to subvert the very laws of nature; a proof of most insolent rashness, to buffet not only with us, but with nature also." (Excerpts from Homily XXVI, 1 Corinthians 11:2-16)

6. Augustine (354-430 A.D.)

Augustine, probably the prominent post-apostolic theologian prior to the Reformation, cites 1 Corinthians 11:4,7 with regard to men: "'Every man praying or prophesying with veiled head shameth his head;' and, 'A man ought not to veil his head, for so much as he is the image and glory of God.'" Now if it is true of a man that he is not to veil his head, then the opposite is true of a woman and she is to veil her head.

"We ought not therefore so to understand that made in the image of the Supreme Trinity, that is, in the image of God, as that same image should be understood to be in three human beings; especially when the apostle says that the man is the image of God, and on that account removes the covering from his head, which he warns the woman to use, speaking thus: 'For a man indeed ought not to cover his head, forasmuch as he is the image and glory of God; but the woman is the glory of the man.'"

B. Reformers and Theologians
1. John Knox (1505-1572)

"First, I say, the woman in her greatest perfection was made to serve and obey man, not to rule and command him. As saint Paule doth reason in these wordes: 'Man is not of the woman, but the woman of the man. And man was created for the cause of the woman, but the woman for the cause of man; and therfore oght the woman to have a power upon her head,' (that is, a coverture in signe of subjection)."

Knox quotes Chrysostom in total harmony: "Even so, (saith he) oght man and woman to appeare before God, bearing the ensignes of the condition whiche they have received of him. Man hath received a certain glorie and dignitie above the woman; and therfore oght he to appeare before his high Majestie bearing the signe of his honour, havinge no coverture upon his heade, to witnesse that in earth man hath no head.' Beware Chrysostome what thou saist! thou shalt be reputed a traytor if Englishe men heare thee, for they must have my Sovereine Lady and Maistresse [Queen Elizabeth]; and Scotland hath dronken also the enchantment and venom of Circes [the enchantress in *The Odyssey* who turned the companions of Odysseus into swine with a magic drink], let it be so to their owne shame and confusion. He procedeth in these wordes, 'But woman oght to be covered, to witnesse that in earth she had a head, that is man.' Trewe it is, Chrysostome, woman is covered in both realmes, but it is not with the signe of subjection, but it is with the signe of superioritie, to witte, with the royal crowne." ("The First Blast Of The Trumpet Against The Monstrous Regiment Of Women," *Works of John Knox*, David Laing, ed. Edinburgh: Printed for the Bannatyne Club, IV:377, 392) The antiquated spelling in this quote comes directly from the original text.

2. John Calvin (1509-1564)

This great theologian of the Reformation preached three sermons from 1 Corinthians 11:2-16 and the following are excerpts:

"So if women are thus permitted to have their heads uncovered and to show their hair, they will eventually be allowed to expose their entire breasts, and they will come to make their exhibitions as if it were a tavern show; they will become so brazen that modesty and shame will be no more; in short they will forget the duty of nature. . . . So, when it is permissible for the women to uncover their heads, one will say, 'Well, what harm in uncovering the stomach also?' And then after that one will plead [for] something else: 'Now if the women go bareheaded, why not also [bare] this and [bare] that?' Then the men, for their part, will break loose too. In short, there will be no decency left, unless people contain themselves and respect what is proper and fitting, so as not to go headlong overboard."

"When he says 'her hair is for a covering (1Cor.11:15 GLP)' he does not mean that as long as a woman has hair, that should be enough for her. He rather teaches that our Lord is giving a directive that He desires to have observed and maintained. If a woman has long hair, this is equivalent to saying to her, 'Use your head covering, use your hat, use your hood; do not expose yourself in that way!"

3. Matthew Henry (1662-1714)

"The woman, on the other hand, who prays or prophesies with her head uncovered dishonoreth her head [1Cor.11:5-6 GLP], namely, the man, v.3. She appears in the dress of her superior, and throws off the token of her subjection. She might, with equal decency, cut her hair short, or cut it close, which was the custom of the man in that age. This would be in a manner to declare that she was desirous of changing sexes, a manifest affectation of that superiority which God had conferred on the other sex."

"She ought to have power on her head, because of the angels [1Cor.11:10]. Power, that is, a veil, the token, not of her having the power or superiority, but being under the power of her husband, subjected to him, and inferior to the other sex."

"It was the common usage of the churches for women to appear in public assemblies, and join in public worship, veiled; and it was manifestly decent that they should do so. Those must be very contentious indeed who would quarrel with this, or lay it aside." (*Matthew Henry's Commentary on the Whole Bible*, McLean, VA: MacDonald Publishing Co., 1706, VI:561, 562)

4. Henry Alford (1810-1871)

"[1Cor.11] 2-16. The law of subjection of the woman to the man (2-12), and natural decency itself (13-16), teach that women should be veiled in public religious assemblies."

"The women overstepped the bounds of their sex, in coming forward to pray and to prophesy in the assembled church with uncovered heads. Both of these the Apostle disapproved, as well their coming forward to pray and to prophesy, as their removing the veil: here however he blames the latter practice only, and reserves the former till ch. xiv. 34."

"The woman ought to have power (the sign of power or subjection; shewn by the context to mean a veil)." (*Alford's Greek New Testament*, Grand Rapids, MI: Guardian Press, 1976), II:563, 564, 566)

5. Frederick Godet (1812-1900)

The phrase [in 1Cor.11:4] "'having down from the head,' that is to say, wearing a kerchief in the form of a veil coming down from the head over the shoulders."

"And since the woman does not naturally belong to public life, if it happen that in the spiritual domain she has to exercise a function which brings her into prominence, she ought to strive the more to put herself out of view by covering herself with the veil, which declares the dependence in which she remains relatively to her husband." (*Commentary on First Corinthians*, Grand Rapids, MI: Kregel Publications, 1977, p. 54, 542)

6. A.R. Fausset (1821-1910)

"In putting away the veil, she puts away the badge of her subjection to man (which is her true 'honor'), and of her connection with Christ, man's Head. Moreover, the head covering was the emblem of maiden modesty before man (Gen. xxiv: 65), and chastity (Gen. xx: 16). By it unlawful excitement in assemblies is avoided, women not attracting attention. Scripture sanctions not the emancipation of woman from subjection: modesty is her true ornament. Man rules; woman ministers: the respective dress should accord. To uncover the head indicated withdrawal from the husband's power; whence a suspected wife had her head uncovered by the priest (Num. v. 18). . . . As woman's hair is given by nature as her covering (v. 15), to cut it off like a man would be palpably indecorous; therefore, to put away the head-covering like a man would be similarly indecorous. It is natural to her to have long hair for her covering: she ought, therefore, to add the other head-covering, to show that she does of her own will that which nature teaches she ought to do, in token of her subjection to man." (A.R. Fausset, *A Commentary, Critical, Experimental, and Practical, on the Old and New Testaments*, Grand Rapids, MI: Eerdmans Publishing Co., 1978, III:II:314)

7. Thomas Charles Edwards (1837-1900)

"It is not improbable that the custom censured by the Apostle was an attempt to symbolize by unveiling the face in public worship the spiritual equality of the woman."

"The man shames his natural head by wearing a veil; that is, he shames himself by wearing a symbol of subjection to the woman, whereas Christ has given the man supremacy over the woman in Church order, and that supremacy is expressed by the symbol of an unveiled face."

"He proves [in 1Cor.11:6 GLP] that a woman that uncovers her head is one and the same with a woman whose head is shorn or shaven. The proof is that woman's long hair is intended by nature and understood by all nations to be a symbol of her subjection to the man. . . . This, the Apostle argues, shows the fitness of the veil to be a symbol of the same subjection in the Christian order. In the Church the veil is added to the symbol of long hair, because the subjection which nature has imposed upon the woman receives a special character when it enters into the Christian series of subordination's."

8. M.R. Vincent

"The head-dress of Greek women consisted of nets, hair-bags, or kerchiefs, sometimes covering the whole head. A shawl which enveloped the body was also often thrown over the head, especially at marriages or funerals. This costume the Corinthian women had disused in the Christian assemblies, perhaps as an assertion of the abolition of sexual distinctions, and the spiritual equality of the woman with the man in the presence of Christ. This custom was discountenanced by Paul as striking at the divinely ordained subjection of the woman to the man." (*A Com-*

mentary on the First Epistle to the Corinthians, first published in 1885, Minneapolis: Klock & Klock Christian Publishers, 1979, pp. 272, 273, 274)

Vincent observes on 1 Corinthians 11:16: "Not the custom of contentiousness, but that of women speaking unveiled. The testimonies of Tertullian and Chrysostom show that these injunctions of Paul prevailed in the churches. In the sculptures of the catacombs the women have a close-fitting head-dress, while the men have the hair short." (*Word Studies in the New Testament*, McLean VA: MacDonald Publishing Co., 1886, II:786, 787)

9. G.G. Findlay

"For a woman to discard the veil means to cast off masculine authority, which is a fixed part of the Divine order, like man's subordination to Christ (3 f.)."

In 1 Corinthians 11:4-5, "the high doctrine just asserted applied to the matter of feminine attire. Since man is man has no head but Christ, before whom they worship in common, while woman has man to own for her head, he must not and she must be veiled. The regulation is not limited to those of either sex who 'pray or prophesy'; but such activity called attention to the apparel, and doubtless it was amongst the more demonstrative women that the impropriety occurred; in the excitement of public speaking the shawl might unconsciously be thrown back."

"And this 'glory' [that is, the glory of the woman's long hair in 1 Corinthians 11:15 GLP] is grounded upon her humility: 'because her hair to serve as a hood (*anti perilolaiou*) has been given her not as a substitute for [the GLP] head-dress (this would be to stultify Paul's contention), but in the nature of a covering, thus to match the veil." (*The Expositor's Greek New Testament*, W. Robertson Nicoll, ed., Grand Rapids, MI: Eerdmans Publishing Co., 1976, II:870, 872, 876)

10. A. T. Robertson (1863-1934)

In commenting on 1 Corinthians 11:4 ("having his head covered"), the renowned scholar of the Greek New Testament observes, "Literally, having a veil (*kalumma*, understood) down from the head."

Paul states in 1 Corinthians 11:6, "Let her be veiled. . . . Let her cover up herself with the veil (down, *kata*, the Greek says, the veil hanging down from the head)."

"It is the sign of authority of the man over the woman. The veil on the woman's head is the symbol of the authority that the man with the uncovered head has over her [1Cor.11:10]." (A.T. Robertson, *Word Pictures in the New Testament*, Nashville, TN: Broadman Press, 1931, IV:159, 160, 161).

11. James Moffat 1870-1944)

"The implication is that as nature has provided woman with a headdress of hair, she is intended, not, of course, to consider this as a substitute for further covering, but to wear a head-dress when she is praying to God in the company of men, nature being regarded as supplying the norm even for such attire." (*The First Epistle of Paul to the Corinthians*, London: Houghter and Stoughton, 1958, 154)

12. W.E. Vine (1873-1949)

"Whatever the character of the covering, it is to be on her head as 'a sign of authority' (v. 10), R.V, the meaning of which is indicated in verse 3 in the matter of headships, and the reasons in verses 7-9, and in the phrase 'because of the angels,' intimating their witness of, and interest in, that which betokens the headship of Christ. The injunctions were neither Jewish, which required men to be veiled in prayer, nor Greek, by which men nor women were alike unveiled. The Apostle's instructions were the 'commandments of the Lord' (14:37) and were for all the churches (vv. 33, 34)." (*Vine's Expository Dictionary of New Testament Words*, 1940)

13. Albrect Oepke (1881-1955)

"The veiling of women is a custom in Israel. A disgraced woman comes veiled to judgment (*katakekalummene*, Sus.32). Yet one may suspect that a woman muffled up (*katekalupsato* to *prosopon*) and lurking by the wayside is a harlot (Gen 38:15). This opens the way for an understanding of the relevant NT passage. The veiling of women in the NT and the contemporary world. In the NT *katakaluptein* occurs only in 1 C. 11:6f in the middle voice. In support of his requirement that women should not pray or prophesy with uncovered heads, Paul appeals to the following considerations of natural law: [Oepke then quotes 1 Corinthians 11:6-7 in Greek]." (*Theological Dictionary of the New Testament*, 1965)

14. John Murray (1898-1975)

"Since Paul appeals to the order of creation (V.3b, v.7ff), it is totally indefensible to suppose that what is in view and enjoined had only local or temporary relevance. The ordinance of creation is universally and perpetually applicable, as also are the implications for conduct arising there from."

"I am convinced that a head covering is definitely in view forbidden for the man (Vs. 4 & 7) and enjoined for the woman (Vs. 5, 6, 15). In the case of the woman the covering is not simply her long hair. This supposition would make nonsense of verse 6. For the thought there is, that if she does not have a covering she might as well be shorn or shaven, a supposition without any force whatever if the hair covering is deemed sufficient. In this connection it is not proper to interpret verse 15b as meaning that the hair was given the woman to take the place of the head covering in view of verses 5,6. The Greek of verse 15 is surely the Greek of equivalence as used quite often in the New Testament, and so the Greek can be rendered: 'the hair is given her for a covering.' This is within the scope of the particular argument of verses 14,15 and does not interfere with the demand for the additional covering contemplated in verses 5,6,13. Verses 14 and 15 adduce a consideration from the order of nature in support of that which is enjoined earlier in the passage but is not itself tantamount to it. In other words, the long hair is an indication from 'nature' of the differentiation between men and women, and so the head covering required (Vs.5,6,13) is in line with what 'nature' teaches."

"On these grounds my judgment is that presupposed in the Apostle's words is the accepted practice of head covering for women in the assemblies of the Church." (Excerpts from a letter to the Evangelical Presbyterian Church of Australia concerning the matter of women being veiled in worship, *Presbyterian Reformed Magazine*, Winter 1992)

15. William Barclay (1907-1978)

Though Barclay's view of the authority of scripture is not orthodox, he too maintains that the covering in 1 Corinthians 11 is a veil: "The problem was whether or not in the Christian Church a woman had the right to take part in the service unveiled. Paul's answer was bluntly this: the veil is always a sign of subjection; it is worn by an inferior in the presence of a superior; now woman is inferior to man, in the sense that man is head of the household; therefore it is wrong for a man to appear at public worship veiled and it is equally wrong for a woman to appear unveiled." (*The Letter to the Corinthians*, Philadelphia: The Westminster Press, 1956, p. 108)

16. J. Vernon McGee (1904-1990)

"Apparently some of the women in the church at Corinth were saying, 'All things are lawful for me, therefore, I won't cover my head.' Paul says this should not be done because the veil is a mark of subjection." (*Thru the Bible with J. Vernon McGee*, Pasadena, CA: Thru The Bible Radio, 1983, V:50)

17. Robert H. Gundry

"Paul's instructions concerning the veiling of women also demand knowledge of prevailing ancient customs. It was proper in the Roman Empire for a respectable woman to veil herself in public. Tarsus, the home city of Paul, was noted for its strict adherence to this rule of propriety. The veil covered the head from view, but not the face. It was at once a symbol of subordination to the male and of the respect which a woman deserves. The Christian women at Corinth, however, were quite naturally following the custom of Greek women, who left their heads uncovered when they worshipped. Paul therefore states that it is disgraceful for Christian women to pray or to prophesy in church services unveiled. On the other hand, Paul goes against the practice of Jewish and Roman men, who prayed with heads covered, by commanding Christian men to pray and prophesy bareheaded as a sign of their authority." (*A Survey of the New Testament*, Grand Rapids, MI: Zondervan Publishing House, 1970, p. 280)

18. Bruce Waltke (1930-present)

"Although Paul does not use the word veil [*kalumma* GLP], it seems reasonable to suppose that he has this article of apparel in view. . . . To appear at the public assembly, then, with inappropriate headdress would disgrace one's head."

"The logical particle 'for' (*gar*) introducing this section [1Cor.11:7-12—GLP] relates it to the preceding statement that improper headdress disgraces one's social head. In 11:7a Paul argues that a veil on a man would disgrace Christ because it would veil the image and glory of God mediated to man through Christ, and in 11:7b-10 he shows that a woman without a veil would in effect be displaying positional equality with the man and would thereby usurp the glory that properly belongs to him by the Creator's design."

"In this writer's judgment, however, it would be well for Christian women to wear head coverings at church meetings as a symbol of an abiding theological truth." ("1 Corinthians 11:2-16: An Interpretation," *Bibliotheca Sacra*, January-March 1978, p.50-51, 57)

19. Gordon Fee (1934-present)

"But what specifically does it mean for the woman to pray and prophesy 'uncovered as to the head'? There are three basic options: (1) The traditional view considered her to be discarding some kind of external covering. This seems to be implied both by the verb 'to cover' and by the words about the man in v. 7, which imply an external covering ('he should not have his head covered'). . . . (2) Because of v. 15, it has been argued that the 'covering' contended for in vv. 4-7 and 13 is actually the long hair of vv. 14-15, because some of the women were having their hair cut short. . . . (3) More recently several scholars have suggested on the basis of the usage in the LXX [Septuagint GLP] that the adjective 'uncovered' refers to 'loosed hair,' that is, to letting her hair down in public and thus experiencing shame. [After critiquing each of the views above, Fee gives his judgment—GLP] On the whole, a modified form of the traditional view [modified in the sense that the covering is a shawl that covers the head, rather than a veil that covers the face GLP] seems to have fewer difficulties, but 'loosed hair' remains a viable option." (*The First Epistle to the Corinthians in The New International Commentary on the New Testament*, F. F. Bruce, ed., Grand Rapids, MI: Eerdmans Publishing Co., 1987, pp. 496, 497) This is not a powerful endorsement, yet Fee still views the covering as fabric rather than hair.

20. Noel Weeks

"There is something ludicrous about being the head or authority while one at the same time hides one's physical head. It follows therefore that praying and prophesying are authoritative functions which call for an unveiled head, unshrouded head. Hence any woman engaging in those activities must also be bare-headed. Consequently Paul turns to what such unveiling must mean for the woman. In contrast to the man, when she prays or prophesies, the unveiling of her head must be dishonorable to her. What does it mean for a woman to be bare-headed? As Paul says, it is equivalent to being shaved or having her hair shorn off. That of course is dishonoring for a woman. Hence she should not uncover her head." (*The Sufficiency of Scripture*, Edinburgh: The Banner of Truth Trust, 1988), pp.129, 130)

21. Robert D. Culver

"God distinguishes sharply between the sexes as to appearance and activity in formal Christian assemblies. A man's hair is to be short and his head uncovered by hat or shawl, while a woman's hair is to be uncut and, in visible recognition of submission to God's order, she is to wear an additional head covering in order to veil, not her face (as in Muslim practice), but some of the rest of her head." (*Women in Ministry: Four Views*, Bonnidell Clouse and Robert G. Clouse, ed., Downers Grove, IL: Inter Varsity Press, 1989, p. 28.)

22. Susan Foh

"The reason for covering heads is directly connected with the headship of the husband; the head is significant here. To suggest some other cultural expression, such as wedding bands to signify the wife's submission to her husband, ignores this integral connection. . . . The discontinuance of coverings for women, by most denominations only in this century, was not done for theological reasons but for cultural reasons (hats went out of style and became too expensive)." (*Women in Ministry: Four Views*, Bonnidell Clouse and Robert G. Clouse, ed., Downers Grove, IL: Inter Varsity Press, 1989, p. 86.)

23. George E. Meisinger

"The term 'uncovered' [in 1Cor.11:5 GLP] consistently refers to taking off some item of clothing; the term 'covered,' [in 1Cor.11:6 GLP] on the other hand, consistently is used of putting on an article of clothing. Either way, when one's head was in view, it was normally used in connection with the ancient veil being a sign of feminine subordination."

"This verse [1Cor.11:6 GLP] shows that the apostle is not talking about the woman growing hair as opposed to putting on an actual head covering of some sort. The verse says that she is without a cover already. Now, if her cover is her hair, it is nonsense to tell her to take off what is already off. If her cover is a hat or veil, however, then it makes sense to tell her to take of her hair, too!" (*The Hat: God's Visual of Headship in Creation*, unpublished, undated, p. 6.)

24. Thomas R. Schreiner

"One of the perplexing questions in this passage is this: What custom regarding adornment is referred to here? We cannot treat this complex question in detail, but the two most probable suggestions can be set forth: (1) the custom Paul recommends is for women to wear shawls. (2) Paul objects to long, loose hair that falls down the back; he wants women to follow the usual custom of piling their hair up on top of their heads. . . . Despite these arguments in favour of the view that Paul is commanding the wearing of hair on top of the head by women, it is probable that Paul is speaking of wearing a head covering of some kind, such as a shawl." ("Head Coverings, Prophecies and the Trinity," *Recovering Biblical Manhood & Womanhood: A Response to Evangelical Femi-*

nism, John Piper and Wayne Grudem, eds., Wheaton, IL: Crossway Books, 1991, pp. 125, 126.)

25. R.C. Sproul (1939-present)

"The problem in Corinth, however, was not that men were prophesying in the public assemblies with their heads covered, but that women were appearing in public assemblies with their heads uncovered. One's dress reflects the principles that one lives by, and that even our exterior must conform to the order that God has established, especially in matters pertaining to public worship.

"The apostle makes the point that the veil, as a symbol of authority, is inconsistent with the position of the man, but it is required for women, who are subordinate to men. If they appear in the public assemblies with their heads uncovered, then they are acting in such a way that challenges the authority of men because they have removed the symbol that they are under masculine authority.

"It is obvious from this comparison between men having their heads uncovered and women having their heads covered, that the covering is not hair. For if the covering in this context were hair, verse 6 would make no sense in the context of this passage."

26. Charles Caldwell Ryrie (1925-present)

"If angels desire to look into things pertaining to salvation, then they should see as they look at veiled women in the assembly of Christians the voluntary submission of a woman to her head. Thus the early church (for this was the custom of the churches generally) while offering religious equality in spiritual privilege insisted on showing in public worship the principle of subordination of women by their being veiled." (*The Role of Women in the Church*, Chicago: Moody Press, 1958, p. 74) (Taken from "Head coverings in Scripture" by Greg Price, http://www.biblebeliever.co.za)

Conclusion

Some of the authors quoted above may disagree on certain issues concerning head coverings, but all agree that Paul was instructing the women to use a fabric, not their long hair, in worship. This conclusion sums up the opinion of apostolic fathers and theologians from different denominational backgrounds and from many periods of church history. The wearing of head coverings in spiritual gatherings was the theological principle and practice of Christian women until the 20th century.

■

Bibliography

Archeological Study Bible	- Zondervan Publications, Grand Rapids, Michigan, 2005
Barnett, Anne	- God's Plan For Godly Women, Everyday Publications Inc., Canada, 2006
Calvin, John	- Calvin's Commentaries, 1st Corinthians & 2nd Corinthians., Wm. B. Eerdmans Publishing Company, 1976
Daniel, Noel	- Did Jesus Rise From The Dead?, GLS Publications, 2009
Daniel, Noel	- Worship & Lord's Supper, S.L.S. Publications, 2004
Elliot, Elizabeth	- Older Women's Mandate, message on CD
Henderson, Warren	- The Fruitful Vine, Gospel Folio Press, 2005
Keener, Craig S.	- The IVP Bible Background Commentary, Inter Vasrsity Press, Downers Grove, Illinois, 1993
Lockyer, Herbert	- All the Women of the Bible, Zondervan publications, Grand Rapids, Michigan, 1967

MacArthur, John	- The Role of Godly Woman, radio message, gty.org
MacArthur, John	- Jesus You Can't Ignore, Thomas Nelson, 2008
Mackay, Harold G.	- Should Christian Women Wear a Head Covering in the Church? Christian Missions Press, Oklahoma
Mackay, Harold G.	- Assembly Distinctives, Everyday Publications Inc.,1981
MacDonald, William	- Believers' Bible Commentary, Thomas Nelson, 1989
Nicholson, J.B. Sr.,	- The Head Covering, Gospel Folio Press, 2006
Ritchie, John	- Focus On the Head-Covering, John Ritchie Ltd, 1996.
Robertson, A.T.	- Word Pictures in the New Testament, Vol.4, Logos Research Systems Publication, 1997
Sproul, R.C.	- Principles against Customs, radio message, Ligonier Ministries.
Wee, Peter	- Women's Head Covering and the Glory of God.

Webliography

http://www.albatrus.org/english/living/modesty/headcoverings_in_scripture.htm

Http://en.wikipedia.org/wiki/Christian_Headcovering

http://members.aol.com/LazerA/headcovering.htm

http://www.kingshouse.org/headcovering.htm

http://www.kingshouse.org/timeline.htm

http://www.foolforhim.com/questions/church/shouldwomenwearheadcoverings.htm

http://www.minthegap.com/2006/10/22/who-wears-the-pants

http://www.backtothebible.org/gateway-to-joy/modesty.html

http://www.gty.org/ Resources/ Transcripts/ 90-219).

http://www.leaderu.com/orgs/cbmw/rbmw/chapter11.html

http://www.frontlinemin.org/women.asp#N_50_

http://www.inthebeloved.org/pdf/am063.pdf)

http://www.biblebeliever.co.za/Brethren/Assemblys/Headcoverings/Scripture/What DoesChurchHistoryTeach.htm

http://gbgm-umc.org/umw/corinthians/veils.stm

http://www.scrollpublishing.com/store/head-covering-history.html